JULY 19

Today I Arrived in Kathmandu

Peter MacFarquhar

SilverWood

Published in 2020 by SilverWood Books

SilverWood Books Ltd
14 Small Street, Bristol, BS1 1DE, United Kingdom
www.silverwoodbooks.co.uk

Copyright © Peter MacFarquhar 2020
Map, 'The Annapurna Circuit' © SilverWood Books
(silverwoodbooks.co.uk)

The right of Peter MacFarquhar to be identified as the author of
this work has been asserted in accordance with the Copyright,
Designs and Patents Act 1988 Sections 77 and 78.

All rights reserved. No part of this publication may be reproduced,
stored in a retrieval system, or transmitted in any form or by any
means, electronic, mechanical, photocopying, recording
or otherwise, without prior permission
of the copyright holder.

This is a work of fiction. Names, characters, places and incidents
either are products of the author's imagination or are used
fictitiously. Any resemblance to actual events or locales
or persons, living or dead, is entirely coincidental.

ISBN 978-1-78132-905-4 (paperback)
ISBN 978-1-78132-906-1 (ebook)

British Library Cataloguing in Publication Data
A CIP catalogue record for this book is
available from the British Library

Page design and typesetting by SilverWood Books
Printed on responsibly sourced paper

PETER MACFARQUHAR evolved into a keen India traveler by a fairly circuitous route. He was originally from New England, but soon moved to South Africa when his parents went there to work. He started school in The Hague in the Netherlands a short time later, and then spent the rest of his childhood and teenage years in Benghazi and Marsa Brega in Libya.

Following the usual order of things, he returned to the United States to attend university, eventually earning an M.A. in TEFL from the University of Hawaii. From there he transferred to the Middle East and worked at a number of universities in the Gulf region for several decades. During this period he took up long distance walking, and began traveling extensively in India, Sri Lanka and Nepal, by train and on foot.

Most of the events described in this book happened during these frequent and wide-ranging journeys. He has recently retired from international education, and now lives in central Florida. He hopes to resume his traveling life in the near future.

Find out more at www.july19kathmandu.com

This book is dedicated to my sons, Gordon and Brooks, and to all of you who encouraged me to write these episodes down, especially Sarah and Cody

July 19: Today I Arrived in Kathmandu

1

Before my driftwood fire I sit,
And see with every waif I burn,
Old dreams and fancies coloring it,
And folly's unlaid ghosts return.

John Greenleaf Whittier

This journey began well. When I was boarding my flight to Nepal in Doha, the airline moved me over to the business section of the plane at no extra charge. That was certainly magnanimous of them. Business class on the airlines of the Gulf is very elegant. They really do indulge you up there in the front. The crew was gracious and attentive. Pink champagne was served as soon as I sat down. The food was delightful and tastefully presented. The wine list was excellent and abundant, and the sweeping views of the deserts below were brilliant. It was one of the most pleasant flights I have ever been on.

Some hours later, as we descended through towering monsoon clouds to land at Tribhuvan International, a large, resplendent rainbow spanned the Kathmandu valley directly across the flight path of the plane. Back on the ground, my arrival proceeded smoothly. My suitcase appeared on the belt quickly, smiling officials waved me right through customs, and on the way in to Thamel, the taxi driver did not blast Bollywood film music, which was something of a minor miracle. I had a good feeling about all this. Things were falling in place rather nicely.

Being newly unemployed, and therefore on a tighter budget than usual, I checked into a convenient, seven-dollar-a-night hotel. This hotel had everything a seven-dollar-a-night hotel could be expected to have: a friendly staff, functioning electricity (more or less), a rudimentary but passable room with an energetic (and noisy) ceiling fan, an attached bath with hot water that was actually hot, and a small balcony. I put the suitcase on a bamboo luggage rack in the corner, and then set about doing the usual sort of settling-in things I often do in budget hotels in the East. I lit some sandalwood incense to take the edge off the slightly dank, rainy-season air in the room. I set up a brace of candles and a box of matches in readiness for the inevitable power cuts to come, tinkered with the leaky plumbing in the bathroom, and rolled out my sleeping bag on top of the bed. (I never get *in* such beds.) I was on the road in the Subcontinent once again.

The room in order, I went out on the balcony and settled into a rickety cane chair with a beedi and a glass of tax-free whisky. This balcony overlooked a courtyard garden awash in besprinkled puddles, rows of luminous orange marigolds, and the sound of falling rain. The rain was slowly increasing.

I really like monsoon time.

2

*The merchandise of gold and silver and precious stones,
and of pearls and fine linen and purple and silk and scarlet,
and of wood and ivory and brass and iron and marble,
and cinnamon and ointments and frankincense,
and beasts and sheep and the bodies and souls of men.*

Revelation 18:12–13

The first order of business was to get a trekking permit. The most beautiful and inspiring regions of Nepal are located in a number of protected natural preserves distributed throughout the country. To enter these areas, you need to apply for an official document showing when you intend to enter and leave the park.

For the most popular and accessible regions like Everest Base Camp, Langtang Valley, and the Annapurna Circuit, these are not expensive and fairly easy to arrange. However, to acquire the permit you have to go over to the government tourist office in person, fill out several forms, provide some passport pictures, and pay the related fees.

Getting to the permit office involved a fairly lengthy crosstown trudge. Thinking to 'save time', I walked there following busy major avenues swollen with the thick traffic, teeming crowds, and bustling street life that Kathmandu is well known for. In the tourist office, I observed again just how friendly and generous the Nepalese people really are. As I was standing at the window filling out the forms, the clerks there cheerfully and very naturally tried to share their lunch with me right over the counter. In how many government offices in capital cities does that happen?

Permit obtained, instead of retracing my steps, I decided to return to my hotel via the narrow streets of the central Kathmandu market. A full-blown Asian bazaar really has to be one of the grandest spectacles on Earth. There are so many things happening in all directions, and at every angle, it approaches visual and mental overload. The shops and the stalls are very small and narrow. There can easily be fifty or sixty of them in less than a stone's throw, providing every conceivable kind of products and goods, and more than a few inconceivable ones as well.

Floating in the breezes above your head to keep them well clear of the monsoon muds below, there are gaze-arresting arrays of glowing fabrics, fluffy wedding dresses, and fiery, gold-embroidered silks. Down at eye level, attached to the walls and hanging on the shop doors, there is any type of merchandise you might desire. You'll find kitchen wares, cast-iron karahis, aluminum kettles, serving vessels and trays of all shapes and uses, suitcases and tote bags, electrical implements, school supplies, woodworking tools, flower vases, locks and keys, backpacks, sleeping bags, trekking equipment, antiques, paintings, handicrafts, carvings, and all manner of bells: smaller models for horses and yaks, and massive, deep-toned versions for temples and monasteries. At knee level there are numerous stands freighted with pyramids of dayglow spices and powders, piles of lentils and beans and rice, tea leaves and herbs, bright yarns in every hue and shade, and incense of all flavors and brands, to note just some of the things that crowd into your view at this height.

Spreading out on the ground there are rafts of plants and trees in small plastic bags, long rows of mats heaped with fruits and vegetables, rubber boots and cheap shoes, umbrellas, combs, prayer beads, stacks of brightly colored plastic buckets and tubs, etc., etc. No available space is unused. And between these profusely bedecked buildings and collaged storefronts, dense floods of humanity press slowly and steadily along, chatting, cruising, laughing, bargaining, hawking, and phoning. There are weather-beaten hill men down from their distant mountain trails, smiling villagers in traditional costumes, hurrying townsmen in suits and ties, serious-looking lamas in maroon robes, ambling children in school uniforms, along with beggars, touts, soldiers, tourists, cyclists, and flute sellers. You name it, it is all part of the ceaseless stream: the rich, multi-faceted East, in all its glory.

This part of town can be dangerous for visitors (such as me) who have not been in a thriving bazaar like this for a while. These people are truly sitting ducks, or rather strolling ones. The chances of them warding off an infectious mania for purchasing, and coming away without a major haul of very cool, must-have junk, are slim. However, one of the benefits of going on walking tours is that you have to carry everything you take with you. This consideration puts a brake on the rampant, shopping-festival atmosphere of the place. It is written: *If you have to carry them, even feathers are heavy.*

3

Like all great travelers,
I have seen more than I remember,
and remember more than I have seen.

Benjamin Disraeli

This was a day of cloudbursts and thunder. The rains began early and continued all day. I stayed in the hotel and sized up my finances. At this stage, I was trying hard to stick to a rather optimistic budget of twenty dollars a day. This state of frugality came about because my job in the Gulf had ended a few weeks previously, and the next chapter of life was not due to start for another six months. I had to live simply and cheaply on the road for half a year.

However, where can you live simply and cheaply on the road in the twenty-first century? That's a good question. This type of long-term traveling existence would have been considerably cheaper and easier to do a few decades ago. If you visited most of the countries in this region in the seventies or the eighties, twenty dollars a day would easily have enabled you to stay in a basic but clean hotel room, with a functional bathroom, a fan, and a mosquito net, eat a substantial meal in a decent restaurant, take rickshaw rides, and drink a few beers. Not exactly wild prodigality, perhaps, but certainly nice enough. To do these things now, you are usually looking at something more like fifty or sixty dollars a day. Times have definitely changed.

In addition, it is not just the prices that have changed. The visa situation in these places is different today as well. Back then, drifting slowly between countries was a lot simpler. Six-month visas were often available for the asking, and they were far less expensive than they are now. And without all the concerns about terrorism that plague modern times, most of these borders were significantly more relaxed, and they were not connected to the internet. Taking advantage of this migration-favoring situation, lots of interesting people were living on the road, making a lifestyle of wandering gradually from one country to another, staying as long as they could in each one, and sometimes rather longer than they expected. Those were lively and colorful times.

Anya was one of these slow travelers, making her way eastward from Europe in a leisurely manner. I met her in Delhi at a rooftop café popular with tourists and hippies. In those days most of the tourists were hippies, come to think of it. She was about twenty years old, good-looking, very bright, idealistic, adventurous, articulate, brave, durable, and musical. Her family was highly talented in the music department. They played five-hundred-year-old Renaissance instruments that they made from scratch in their basement workshop. She was hitch-hiking to India carrying her violin, which must have felt entirely natural coming from a background like that. She told me her story over several rounds of chai.

As it turned out, she had just been released from a five-month stay in the Amritsar municipal jail. Somewhere on the road in Pakistan about half a year prior to this, she had been picked up by a friendly compatriot driving a Volkswagen van, the basic, ubiquitous, go-to mode of transportation of the times. This must have appeared to her like a stroke of good fortune. A long ride, all the way to her destination with someone from her own background, would have been very welcome to a stranded traveler standing alone on the road in the uncertain wilds of Pakistan. However, unbeknownst to her, this van was fitted with a false bottom, concealing a cache of advanced automatic weapons. The driver was not the benevolent, easygoing tourist he was pretending to be at all. He was actually running guns to the separatists in Kashmir. He had picked up Anya to use her as convincing camouflage for crossing the Indian border.

And, as is often the way with such doings, someone in the know had tipped off the Indian border guards about his impending arrival. They were expecting him, and when they got to the border, the guns were quickly discovered. He was promptly arrested, and she was also put in the Amritsar jail, charged with being an accomplice. Eventually, when the driver had duly explained all this to the court, it came out that she was completely innocent and had no involvement with this operation at all. However, the wheels of justice move very slowly in India, and five months passed before she was allowed to leave the jail.

She was handling all of this remarkably well. In spite of this long, arduous stint behind bars, she was quite buoyant, and still keen to keep on traveling. Most people in her situation would have been thoroughly undone by such an ordeal, and desperate to get on the next plane home. When I met her, she was vindicated and in the clear, but she was not free to resume her travels just yet. There was one more thing she had to do. Her passport was still buried somewhere in the murky depths of the Amritsar jail. A short while later, we took a train up there to retrieve it.

The filing 'system' at the Amritsar jail really had to be seen to be appreciated, or even believed. This incident happened well before the advent of the ever-present computers for everything we have now. No doubt the place has been thoroughly modernized since then, but at that time, the jail's clerical department was located in an open courtyard surrounded with arched cloisters of little rooms along the sides. These small chambers were stuffed from floor to ceiling with stacks of manila folders piled up against the walls on all sides, almost burying the small mahogany desk placed in the middle of the floor. At this desk there sat a humble clerk who was responsible for keeping track of the contents of the room.

In these packed-out compartments there was no obvious ordering or retrieval system anywhere to be seen. Instead, the location of every individual folder in there was stored in the head of the resident clerk. He alone had any clue where anything was. This required an impressive feat of super-accurate memory because there were thousands of these folders in each room. This was truly astonishing. Imagine what could happen to you if that clerk was sick, or re-assigned, or, heaven forbid, died? Your file might well never see the light of day again. However, Indian clerks excel at this sort of thing. And fortunately for us, on the day we appeared, the clerk in charge of the room containing Anya's file was sitting at his desk, alive and well, synapses firing. He quickly found her passport in a minute or two of purposeful rummaging, and we were free to go. If it had it been up to me, that man's salary would have been quadrupled immediately.

On our way out to the street, we stopped in front of a crowded cell near the front entrance to say goodbye to the driver of the van. He had been sentenced to three and a half years. Even though this cell was only about twelve by fifteen feet with one narrow, strongly barred door, it held something like twenty inmates. We are talking shades of the Black Hole of Calcutta here. We stood in front of the bars for a bit, while the prisoners inside made way for the driver to come up to the door. He stood there with thick iron shackles around his wrists, chained onto some heavy-duty, medieval-looking leg irons. To his credit, he was very polite and apologetic about having caused the whole mess. We wished him well, gave him what money we could, and headed for the nearby exit. The moral of this brief tale is clear: Don't be running guns into Kashmir for love or money.

As we were going through the prison gates, we passed by a small group of disheartened travelers who had just been brought in from the same border where Anya had been arrested five months before. I have forgotten what most of these understandably worried folks looked like, but one of them stands out clearly in my memory. This was a middle-aged American lady with a large, cone-shaped wicker basket like the ones Nepalese porters use tied to her back. She had modified it with a backpack harness and a hinged wooden lid. It must have been a good hundred and fifty liters or so in volume, and it was jammed full of cats. Nine of them, she said. Now I am pretty sure that most Indian border guards don't see crazy tourists schlepping strapping hampers of stray cats all that often. Nonetheless, I think that they would probably have been okay with it, if a tad incredulous, and allowed her to continue on into Pakistan, baggage intact. However, she had heedlessly overstayed her visa, and there she was, mournfully checking in to the Amritsar municipal jail, hamper and all. These borders were more relaxed back then, but not that relaxed. I don't know what happened to her or the poor cats after that. We didn't hang around to find out. Our overriding thought just then was *let's get out of here before they change their mind.*

Some of these migrants were not quite as innocent as Anya was, however. About a year later, I met another traveler who was also in serious trouble with the authorities because of border irregularities. Very serious trouble in this case. This was Kara from Australia. Kara was traveling back and forth between India and Afghanistan, buying up gemstones, and then smuggling this loot out of the country. At that time, tourist visas for Afghanistan were a bit shorter than they were in some of the other countries in that region. They let you stay there for around a month, I think it was, but if you wanted to extend your visit beyond that, you usually had to leave for a while and then come back on a clean slate. This was easier and faster, and more likely, than trying to get a visa extension in-country.

This enterprising traveler found these restrictions inconvenient for her business activities. To bypass them, she always traveled with two passports, one from Australia and the other from the UK. And, somehow or other she had managed to acquire a real, date-adjustable visa stamp from passport control. I am not sure whether she had bribed someone, or if she had pilfered it on her way into the country, or what, but she had one. She would first enter Afghanistan legally on one of her passports, and stay for as long as she wanted to. Then, whenever she decided that it was time to leave, she would neatly enter a completely authentic-looking visa stamp in her other passport, pencil in a suitable arrival date, and casually depart, with no one the wiser.

Kara had prospered under this clever arrangement for several years, but eventually the Afghan authorities figured out what she was doing, and the halcyon days of this lucrative scheme came to an abrupt halt. Early one morning, undercover agents arrested her at her hotel, and clapped her into the formidable Kabul central prison for a good long time. This was a massive, gloomy, seriously scary fortress. Things must have been really heavy in there. The Russians invaded the country not long after that, and Lord knows what happened to her in the upheavals that followed. These are not countries to get in trouble in. There really is much to be said for staying home and just seeing some of these areas on TV. Once you are behind bars here, you are well and truly buried. If you do go, it is wise to tread very carefully in such places.

The border she had been taking these cavalier liberties with was the one between Afghanistan and Pakistan in the historic Khyber Pass. Doing a visa run here involved getting up really early in the morning in either Peshawar or Kabul, and boarding the special bus bound for the frontier. This bus would take you part of the way through the Khyber Pass and stop at the border. There you had to get off, walk through the passport control areas on both sides, and then get on a second bus in the other country to complete the transit. These visa runs usually took us a whole day.

This borderland was a fascinating region. The bus usually made several stops in some of the villages and towns along the way for tea, bathroom breaks, and lunch. One of the last villages on the Pakistani side was a little place called Landi Kotal. We normally stayed there for about thirty minutes or so, and while the driver and most of the other passengers sat around chatting and smoking beedis in the tea stalls, I would wander off and have a look around.

One of the shops in this village had bricks of hash the size of bread pans casually stacked outside the door, like so much firewood. And they could well have been firewood, for all anybody noticed or cared. No one except me paid any attention to them at all. If a whole brick was beyond your requirements, this shop also provided smaller amounts that looked a lot like thick, brown mosquito coils: marketing strategies, North-West Frontier style.

The next shop down from this one displayed a broad selection of fresh produce like eggplants, tomatoes, cucumbers, lemons, garlic, and onions. And sitting prominently in the middle of the vegetables was a large wooden crate filled with loose ammunition of the Lee Enfield and Kalashnikov varieties, along with a smattering of Colt .45 rounds and an assortment of shotgun shells. Interested customers picked through the box and selected the cartridges they wanted one at a time, just like they would do with the onions and the tomatoes in the cartons next to them. The winds of supply and demand are seldom still in these parts.

While I stood there marveling over this pile of ammo, a business-minded local boy about nine years old came up to me, decked out in the standard tribal area costume: brown charwal-chemise, an embroidered vest, a flat, commander Massoud-style woolen hat, a shoulder blanket, and the usual heavy-duty, border region sandals. He looked for all the world like a miniature Taliban fighter, which he may well have grown up to become.

He offered me a range of curious wares, beginning with a sizeable slab of dark hash. When I had politely declined this, he brought out a collection of tiny glass vials of German medical cocaine, which I turned down as well. Understanding that I was not looking to score drugs, he changed tactics. He then produced a fat wad of assorted currencies and asked if I would like to change any money. When I informed him that I didn't require this service either just then, he offered me what at first glance appeared to be a large, old-fashioned fountain pen. After a closer examination, however, this turned out to be a cleverly disguised gun that fired a single .22 caliber bullet. I hadn't been expecting that one. Where on earth does a nine-year-old kid from the north-west tribal area get a commercial supply of pharmaceutical cocaine from Europe, thick stacks of foreign cash, and lethal James Bond hardware? Not a big deal in Landi Kotal, it would appear.

After stopping in Landi Kotal, the bus continued on its way to the end of Pakistani territory, where we were to get off and proceed on foot over to the Afghan side. When we arrived at the border, a traveler who had been sitting somewhere in the back got out carrying an enormous, antique blunderbuss he had picked up on a back street in Peshawar. I couldn't decide if this was a real antique or not. The local gunsmiths in Peshawar are highly skilled at turning out some very authentic-looking fakes. But real or not, this thing had been handsomely and artistically made. It had a beautifully carved and finely polished hardwood stock, and a heavy, octagonal barrel that was neatly inlaid with brass, floral designs. It was a rare piece of work, rather like its owner. He got off the bus, leaned the gun on his shoulder, and then marched rigidly over the line, imitating an elite soldier on full dress parade, beaming a serene, complete-nutcase smile all the way. It is truly remarkable what a few months of prime Indian ganja can do to your grip on reality. Crossing the Khyber Pass may have been time-consuming, but it was never dull.

Anyway, that was a different era. Nowadays the countries in this region are considerably more expensive, these borders are a lot stricter and smarter, and the travelers are cut from a different cloth. I put my feet up on the balcony, and pondered the changes while the heavy rains thrummed on the flagstones below.

4

A man must stand on the side of a hill with his mouth open for a long time before a roast duck flies in.

Chinese proverb

It had been a while since I had tried to live on the road like this. In recent decades, whenever I have gone out for a bit of a walkabout, I have always been a short-term tourist taking a temporary break from the usual routine and the job. This time around I was more of a long-term traveler. A number of very skillful commentators have articulated the differences between tourists and travelers, so I seriously doubt that I have anything terribly original to add to that discussion. Basically, if there really is a difference, for me it would be that tourists have jobs and lives somewhere else that they are planning to return to fairly soon. And in addition to returning to the same lives, most tourists come back from their journeys the same people they were when they left. But with travelers, the journey they are currently on is the only life they have, and they are often going through personal changes. Things tend to be in flux with them. But not to put too fine a point on it, perhaps this is not such a meaningful distinction. However, going in one mode or the other does seem to produce a different type of road karma. My older sister has a knack for expressing large concepts with only a few words. One of her more proverbial encapsulations was: *You meet what you are.* I think there might be some truth in this. I tend to meet a different type of people, and I seem to have different kinds of experiences, when I am not a tourist, as we shall see.

In the meantime, there were a series of small errands that needed doing. I had to round up a few better-to-have-with-you bits and pieces still missing from the trail kit: hand sanitizer, comb, soap, gloves, scarf, and so forth. Also, during the summer months in this region, it is a good idea to avoid eating things like salads, the garnishes on plates, and any vegetables that have not been vigorously cooked.

This plan will help you to avoid many of the stomach disorders, the assorted parasites, and the runs that often afflict the tourists here. However, this policy also tends to slant your diet rather heavily towards carbs, which is not really a healthy way to eat for too long.

A good way to counteract this imbalance is to eat fresh fruits and vegetables with skins you can peel, such as bananas, apples, oranges, tangerines, cucumbers, papayas, and mangos, whenever you can find them. However, peeling some of these things can be rather messy and difficult to get right if you only have a small pocket knife to hand. This operation works far more smoothly if you use a decent vegetable peeler. One of these was on the must-get list as well, and I was soon off to the bazaar once again. Back there in the street, I carefully picked my way between the puddles, trying to avoid the mud splashing from charging rickshaws, careless motorcycle riders, and hard-stomping porters.

While I was attending to these errands, I was trying to break in a pair of new hiking boots as well. The last pair I had took off several of my toenails after only a few days on the PCT (Pacific Crest Trail), and were subsequently donated to the Goodwill store in Reno, Nevada when I came down from the trail. Hiking boots that take off your toenails in less than a week are not keepers.

Actually, this unpleasant result was not completely the fault of the boots. When I started out on the PCT, my intention was to walk about five to seven miles a day for the first week or so, and get used to it slowly. I adhered to this plan conscientiously for about five days. But on the next day, I fell in with a crew of articulate, friendly hikers an hour before I reached my daily limit, and started walking along with them. They were heading for a campsite that was another fifteen miles farther on. Having now been on the trail for several months, these people were super-fit, and a distance like this was nothing for them. And so, without thinking about what I was doing, I carried on with them, chatting easily and continuously about this and that, and the extra miles quickly flew by. However, by the time we arrived at their campsite some hours later, the damage was done. I had acquired a major array of serious blisters, several nails were beginning the process of coming off, and by the next morning I was almost a cripple. Believe me, that standard advice about taking time to break yourself in to the rigors of long-distance trails is something you ignore at your peril. I was hoping that wearing the new boots all over town before hitting the trail in them would help prevent something like that from happening again. In the event it did not, but more about that anon.

On the way to the bazaar, and then again on the way back, I was accosted by a steady succession of aggressive touts and a mixed array of beggars and con men. Exchanges with the touts and the beggars were usually brief:

Street Person: Namaste!
Me: No.

End of story.

The interactions with the con men were somewhat more involved. These guys would step out of a side street or an alley as I went by, and fall into step near me, trying hard to give the impression that they just happened to be walking in the same direction at the same time. Then, after about a hundred meters or so, they would nonchalantly initiate a conversation that usually went something like this:

Street Person: How are you, Sir?
Me: Fine, thanks.
Street Person: Very nice shoes, Sir!
Me: Thank you.
Street Person: Where did you get them?
Me: At home.
Street Person: Where is your home, Sir?

Me: America.

Street Person: Oh, very good country, Sir.

Me: Thank you.

Street Person: Is America like Nepal?

Me: No, it's quite different.

Street Person: Really? Let me take you to a famous temple.

Me: Actually, I am a bit busy now. No, thanks.

Street Person: Very old, Sir. Very special. Good for karma!

Me: No, thank you.

Street Person: I don't want money, Sir. Just practice English.

Me: Please leave me alone.

Street Person: Buy milk for my baby, Sir. Baby very hungry.

Me: Please go away.

Street Person: Here is a cheap shop, Sir. Only milk, Sir.

Me: Tell you what: let's ask this policeman about that.

Zoom, gone.

The funny thing about these conversations was that almost all of these characters said the same things, and almost always in the same order, as if they had gone to a special school for it. That well-rehearsed, conversational lead-in had clearly been planned with some skill. I half expected to discover old Fagin himself reviewing the situation from an upstairs window. Now I don't mind buying a can of powdered milk for a starving tot, and I will do, now and again. But when these same little rituals start being repeated on a daily basis, it tends to bring out the curmudgeon within. And besides, the hungry tot probably doesn't exist. And even if there actually is a starving baby somewhere in the picture, the poor thing would most likely never see the milk anyway. That will be sold on for cash within a few minutes. I don't like having to be short with unfortunate, struggling people, but some of these con artists can really be pests.

As so often happens in these parts, I returned from the bazaar with several things that were not on the list. Outside my room there was a pleasant rooftop garden with assorted pots of flowers and shrubs and a cactus or two. I contributed a small pomegranate tree that I found in the bazaar. This was sitting forlorn and neglected and covered with thick dust in a little plastic bag on one of the crowded market streets, in considerable danger of being stomped underfoot. Spending a dollar to rescue it had seemed like the right thing to do. I also bought several tubes of sunblock and toothpaste, and a blue and red cotton lunghi to wear for pajamas. Sleeping in the same clothes you walk in may save you some weight, but this is not really a good idea, especially in the summertime during the leech season.

I was now phasing into walking mode, making final preparations and last-minute arrangements. My hotel was conveniently located right in the center of things in the main tourist area, but there was one major feature that it didn't have: double-locked security boxes to leave your important documents and valuables in while you are off walking in the hills. The reception desk told me that these had been destroyed during the recent earthquake. It is not wise to wander on high, remote trails wallet a-bulge with cash and plastic. After breakfast I went out and located another hotel nearby (right across the street, in fact) that did have that kind of deposit boxes. This new hotel was fifteen dollars a day, which would scupper my modest budget, but I decided that this was really necessary.

I also thought it would be a good idea to visit the long-distance minibus station and nail down where I needed to be to catch an early ride to the trailhead. It is far better to figure this out in daylight hours beforehand than to attempt it at four or five a.m. in the dark. It is easy to get lost in the intricate mazes of small side streets and winding lanes in Kathmandu. I took a taxi over to the bus station to sort this out after making arrangements for the hotel shift later in the day.

After lunch I rounded up my stuff and moved to the other hotel across the street that had the reliable security boxes in their luggage room. Sitting on the floor in that room a little while later, it didn't take long to see that once again, I had brought way too much baggage. I had arrived in Nepal thinking I would save money by camping out along the trail. However, this was not a realistic scheme. Sleeping outdoors in the monsoon rain is not very pleasant, and the lodges in the hills only cost one or two dollars a night, which would not really amount to all that much saving. In addition, I was now way too out of shape to carry the camping gear comfortably anyway. I decided to leave it behind in the luggage room instead, and sat on the threadbare carpet reorganizing the load.

5

The end of the fight is a tombstone white,
with the name of the newly deceased,
And an epitaph drear that says a fool lies here,
who tried to hustle the East.

Rudyard Kipling

Today was my birthday. Another year had passed already. It is truly remarkable how quickly they flash by these days. An entire year now feels about as long as two or three months used to. Dotage draws on apace, eternity beckons, the grave looms.

Speaking of the passage of time, one of the first things you notice here is that folks in the East have a different sense of this than people in most Western lands do. They take a different approach; they are in another zone. In the West, efficiency is viewed as one of the most sacred of the sacred cows. And there really is much to be said for getting things done rapidly and well, for accurate schedules that really happen, and for punctuality you can depend on. This is what most Westerners are wired to expect, even when they are trying hard not to be.

As such, one of the common mistakes that many new visitors to countries in the Subcontinent often make is they try to pack far too much into a short time frame, expecting that everything will just flow seamlessly from one event to the next. Understandably, they have come a long way at a great expense, and they want to make the most of their time here. They often arrive with ambitious expectations and dynamic schedules and long lists of things to do, places to visit, and sights that must be seen, without 'wasting any time'. First, they are going to do a bit of trekking, and then they are going to go rhinoceros watching on a jungle safari. After that they plan to fit in a rafting trip, go tour some temples and monasteries, attend a few meditation and yoga classes, and then wind things up with several days of mega shopping in Kathmandu, all within the space of about two weeks, or even less than that.

What these folks soon start to discover is that greater India just doesn't move like this. When you glide into the Subcontinent on a triple seven from the other side of the world, you are usually moving much too fast internally to mesh with the local pace of things. As a result, it is really easy to just rush past a lot of fascinating, unfolding scenes and details that you will only notice if you are going slowly enough. They miss much of the magic of India because they are moving too fast to see it. You have to slow down. In these parts, less really is more.

I learned this gradually, and largely by accident over the course of a number of journeys, most of which were way too rushed. On one trip, I landed in Jodhpur in Rajasthan, and set out on a circular route through Jaisalmer, Bikaner, Jaipur, Ajmer, and Udaipur designed to bring me back around to the Jodhpur airport to catch the flight home about ten days later. According to this schedule, I had to keep moving steadily, spending at most a day or two in each place, and then get right back on the road.

Near the end of the trip, I arrived in Udaipur, the city with the romantic and astronomically expensive hotel in the middle of the lake. Here I encountered a logistical problem. Jodhpur and the airport were still about a day's journey farther on. However, there was no train link between these two cities, as I had naively assumed there was. As a rule, I always try to avoid the government buses, having learned the hard way just what a grinding experience such rides can turn into. But here I had no choice. Taking the government bus was the only option that fit into my slender time frame. Early in the morning, I bought a bus ticket and mustered up the nerve to face the solid masses of bodies, the tiny, rigid seats, the unhappy babies, the awkward, intrusive bundles, the fingernails on the chalkboard movie music, and the non-stop horn. In short, I voluntarily signed on for twelve hours of ordeal-by-planning.

But what a fortuitous event this dreaded bus ride turned out to be. About halfway between the towns of Udaipur and Jodhpur there is a prominent tableland that is a bit less than a hundred kilometers wide, and about a kilometer higher than the surrounding plains. Incidentally, this plateau also contains the Kumbhalgarh fortress, one of the largest in India, and said to have the second-longest wall in the world after the Great Wall of China. Because of its elevation, and the absence of decent roads, this expansive upland has historically been a difficult place to get to. As a result of its limited accessibility, time stood still in this region while the plains below modernized and moved on, leaving what is up there in something of a time warp.

This is an out-of-the-way pastoral zone, irrigated by creaking, wooden water wheels, with ancient sugar cane presses driven by bullocks with painted and beflowered horns, a few tiny roads about the width of a sidewalk, and hardly any cars. The bus crept slowly onward, passing troupes of villagers working in the fields in their bare feet. These hill women were wrapped in shining saris of the same emerald green colors, and embroidered with the same yellow flowers as the ones in the fields they were cultivating. As they moved along through the crops, it looked like the fields were walking. There was very little sound other than their cheerful voices wafting over the land.

It was only as we were inching down the narrow track on the far side of this mesa that I understood what I had just fleetingly glimpsed and missed: a rare pocket of old India as it had been about eighty years ago, the truly magical India that so many of us go there hoping to find. I had blasted (relatively speaking) right past where I really wanted to be. This is what schedule worship and too much momentum can do to your travel experiences here.

To redeem myself, I made a second trip back to

this enchanting region during another school break later on. On this occasion, I met a wraith-like, seventy-something-ish British woman of the old school who was staying at a simple hotel in a village close to the Kumbhalgarh fort. She had grown up in India during the last days of the Raj, and knew all about going slow. She was spending a month traveling with the camel caravans that carry raw sugar from farms on the plateau down to the towns of the plains. When I described my intention to spend a few days exploring the area, she wagged a long, bony finger in my face and firmly ordered: *Now you just settle down there, Sonny, and do this thing right!* (I was about forty at the time.) In her well-seasoned view, I was still moving much too fast to connect with the place properly.

At this point, I had grasped something about the need to slow down, but I still didn't understand how one actually did this exactly. In former times, many India travelers accomplished this internal down-shift by smoking lots and lots of ripping weed, but this method did not appeal to me. However, I caught a major hint in this direction on yet another India trip a year or two later.

On this occasion I was wandering around in Tamil Nadu on the trains, exploring southern India with one of my children. As you know, young children often come down with assorted ailments such as fevers, diarrhea, stomach troubles, vomiting, and the like, and most parents tend to become fairly inured to all this after a few seasons. Coping with these things just becomes a standard part of the parenting landscape. Symptoms of this sort occurring by themselves are usually not a big deal, and they will normally pass on their own. But if a child has a high fever, and diarrhea, and is vomiting, all at the same time, you can be in serious trouble, particularly when you are on the road in the interior of India. Nasty things like cholera and typhoid usually begin with these same symptoms, and my son was exhibiting all three of them. It was clearly urgent to get him off that train and start some proper treatment right away. We bailed out at the next station, and found a reasonably clean hotel room with a tolerable attached bath and a working AC. I put him into bed, plied him with glasses of cola and juice, started him on a course of antibiotics (I never travel without them), and settled down to await the result.

Once he had fallen peacefully asleep, I went out to investigate where we actually were. And lo and behold, yet another wonderfully serendipitous 'accident' had occurred. We had landed in a small temple town well off the beaten track in another one of those vanishing pockets of magical, old India. As an insightful and articulate person somewhere out there has observed (I have tried repeatedly but unsuccessfully to find out who composed this sentence): *Three hundred years of colonialism did less damage than thirty years of tourism.* This small town was almost completely untouched by the tourism onslaught that has engulfed so much of the rest of the country.

With the patient slumbering alone back at the hotel, I didn't want to go too far afield, so I poked around a bit in the areas nearby. First, I stepped into a large temple complex just down the street where a major religious festival was then underway. Inside there were hundreds of townsfolk and villagers standing five abreast in a long line awaiting their turn to present incense and prayers in the inner sanctum. And down the whole length of a long wall right in back of them, there was a very realistic, life-sized mural of the exact same scene that had been painted hundreds of years before. The folks standing in the line looked just like the figures painted on the wall behind them, with the same postures, the same clothes, the same strings of flowers, the same colors, and the same expressions. It was as if the people painted on the wall had come back to life. The entire setting effused a pervading and transporting sensation of timelessness.

Hard by this temple there was an old, stone bridge spanning a shallow river with a single, pointed arch about seventy-five yards long. The narrow lane that crossed it was barely three yards wide. On both sides of this small throughway there was a raised sidewalk about a foot and a half higher than the rest of the roadbed. And on these sidewalks, there were lines of villagers sitting cross-legged on plaited reed mats, selling small amounts of things like chilis, ginger, garlic, herbs, onions, tomatoes, and salad greens. I sat down with these simple vendors, and rested against the time-scarred stones.

What a find! A large swath of rural India was pouring steadily over the bridge. This parade was so close to me I could have reached out and touched it. I was just about in it. There were no cars. Everyone was on foot, or rolling gently forward on carts and bicycle rickshaws. There were hand-drawn school carriages full of small children coming back from classes, sedan chairs ferrying plump, bejeweled rich people away from town, ox carts creeping along piled with melons and coconuts and hay, reeking fish wagons, street vendors carrying all manner of wares, craftsmen with canvas bags of tools, be-smutched construction workers lugging long sections of rusty rebar on their shoulders, vegetable sellers balancing large baskets of produce on their heads, clerks with briefcases and bright red bhindis splashed across their foreheads, water buffaloes pulling heavy loads of thick, dark timbers, shepherds leading flocks of small, skinny goats, strolling musicians, and the occasional free-ranging bull wandering past in the evening light. I leaned back on the wall, and let this spellbinding river of humanity flow by.

And then came the eureka moment. *This* was how you slowed down. On all of my previous trips, I had always gone out energetically searching for the magic of India, resolutely attempting to track it down wherever it was, in a restless, unsatisfying treasure hunt that was not very successful. I did encounter a few scattered glimpses of this fleeting apparition here and there, but the full vision always seemed to elude me. And now, here it was, the whole rich tapestry of small-town Indian life, gently washing over me, bending its steps slowly homewards in the closing of the day. This was a revelation, a whole new approach: *Be still, and let the magic of the land come to you.* And it will, very often, if not usually, when you are least expecting it, in accordance with the Zen of finding things.

Back at the hotel, after a few days of rest and rehydration, the amoxicillin had done its work. The adverse symptoms had dissipated, normal appetites returned, and my ailing son was now fit to travel once again. We had before us a day and a night of riding the rails over the Southern Ghats back to Trivandrum to get the flight home to Oman. We bought our tickets, loaded up the picnic basket, and boarded the late-afternoon train.

Just before sundown the train slowed as we came into an isolated country town. About two hundred meters before the station, a sizeable crowd of young girls was assembled next to the tracks. They were all wearing traditional, brightly colored, be-mirrored Indian dresses, and they were carrying sturdy brass water pots in their arms. In the sinking sun, the tiny mirrors on their clothing shone like rubies, and their brass pots were aglow in deep gold. As the train was slowing down, the girls assaulted it en masse before it stopped, and rushed headlong into the bathrooms up and down the train.

This was an efficient, well-practiced operation. They had clearly done this before, and they knew exactly what they were doing. This place had a serious water problem. Their mission was to grab as much water as they could from the bathrooms before the train pulled out. It was a near riot. This gang of exuberant, determined children romped through the carriages, loudly slamming the doors and banging the pots, chattering and shouting, with explosions of laughter and water noises, as we looked on agog.

I think the children thought we were going to be there for longer than we were, but we barely stopped. In the middle of this rowdy water fest, the train started pulling out of the station. I suspect that the driver knew what was afoot, and stepped on the gas to curtail it as soon as he could. *Ain't nobody steals water from my train.* As a result, quite a few of these children were still on board when we began to move, and they panicked. In a flash, grasping the danger of the situation, a number of us passengers rushed to the doors and started swinging these sparkling water thieves and their shining pots into the sunset. Fortunately, no one was injured. They all made it off the train safely, and most of the water did too.

As the train sped on into the gathering darkness, we stretched out in our sleeper berths with a mixture of feelings: surprise and disbelief at the completely unexpected and improbable nature of the whole scene; sympathy for the children and the harsh life that was forcing them to do this; gratitude that no one was injured, deeply touched by the twilight beauty of this unique and unimaginable moment. The magic of India finds you, not the other way around, if you slow down.

*

This was my last day in Kathmandu before heading to the Annapurna region about two hundred and fifty kilometers away in the middle of the country. I spent what was left of the afternoon deciding which stuff to leave behind in the luggage room. I put the extra cash, the cards, and the plane tickets into the security box, arranged for a pre-dawn taxi, and took a bath, mindful that it might be a while before I saw hot water again. Showered and shaved, I went back to the street and put a Nepali SIM card in my phone, and sent a few messages to my family informing them where I was going. And then I sat down to a hearty Italian dinner in the much beloved La Dolce Vita restaurant, and went to bed early to be ready for departure in the wee hours.

6

Annapurna
Goddess of the Harvests.

The mountain

The Annapurna region is a large massif in the northern part of central Nepal, about a day's drive west of Kathmandu. This area contains some of Nepal's most famous and scenic great mountains. The list includes Machhapuchhre, 'The Fish's Tail', and Annapurna, which, topping out at about eight thousand and one hundred meters, is one of the highest mountains in the world. It is situated between two other prominent, huge peaks, Dhaulagiri and Manaslu.

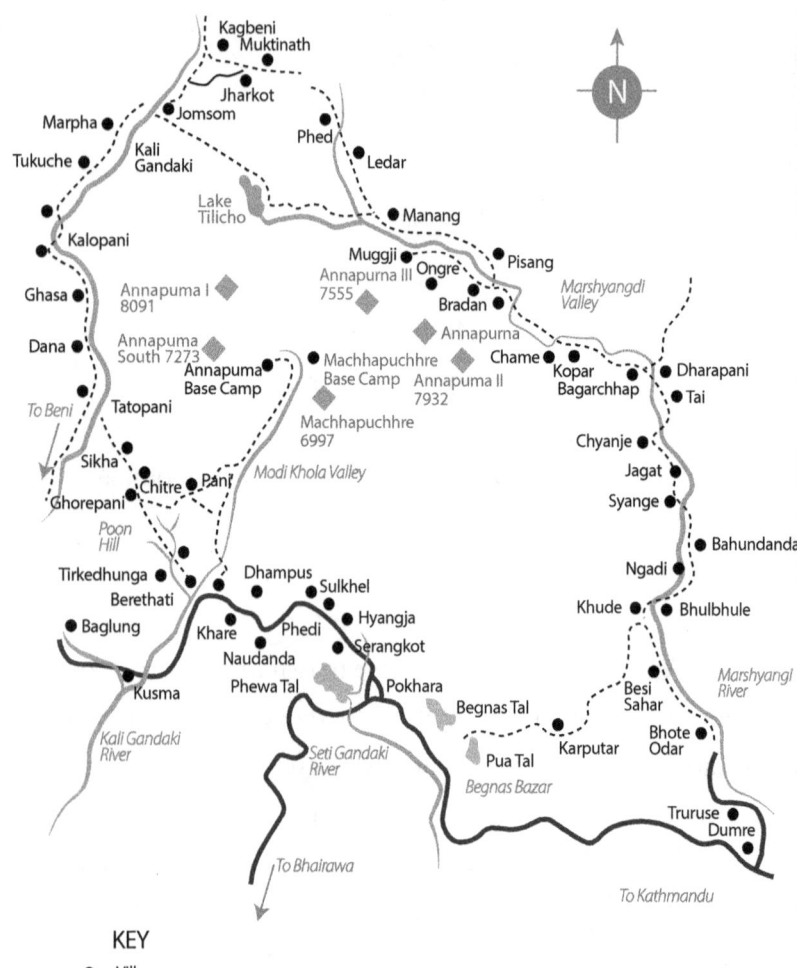

The Annapurna massif is also one of the main Himalayan landmarks you can see as you fly in to the country if you are sitting on the north side of the plane. This towering edifice is more than thirty miles wide, and it is demarked by the Kali Gandaki River on its western side (this is one of the deepest gorges in the world), and by the Marsyangdi River valley on the eastern side. The pleasant, lakeside city of Pokhara, the second-largest town in Nepal, is just to the south of it, and is often used as a convenient and comfortable base for climbing expeditions and treks into this upland region.

Annapurna was the first eight-thousand-meter mountain to be climbed. Maurice Herzog and his French teammates made the first ascent in June, 1950. They had come to this area intending to climb Dhaulagiri, the massive peak on the western side of the Kali Gandaki Gorge. However, after several weeks of exploration, they had not been able to find a suitable route on that mountain, and they turned their attention to Annapurna across the valley.

Ascents of these great mountains have to be made after the winter ends, but before the highly dangerous monsoon weather conditions set in around the beginning of June. This is not a very big window. During the last few weeks before the monsoon arrived,

Herzog and his team set out on what was intended to be a reconnaissance of Annapurna. Their maps were not very good, and they experienced considerable difficulties and delays in just locating it. However, when they got to the base of the mountain, the weather was still good. Even though they were not yet completely equipped for a full-scale ascent, they decided to attempt a lighter, alpine-style dash for the summit. They succeeded in reaching the top right before the monsoon broke, but their horrendous descent nearly killed them. They missed the correct path down, they lost their gloves and their goggles, they suffered badly from snow blindness, they couldn't find their tents, they had to spend a freezing night shivering in a crevasse, and so forth. The summit party ended up losing many of their fingers and almost all of their toes from severe frostbite (which, incidentally, did not prevent Herzog from eventually serving as mayor of Chamonix after he had recovered back in France). Considering how lightly equipped and provisioned they were when they launched this last-minute ascent, this was a remarkable achievement.

In the decades since then, Annapurna has recorded one of the highest percentage of fatalities per climbing attempts on any of the world's eight-thousand-meter giants. Thirty-four percent of the people who have tried to climb Annapurna have died doing it, which is quite similar to the percentage of deaths on famously dangerous K2 in Pakistan. This is a formidable mountain. For those who are interested in this kind of Himalayan lore, Herzog's lively account of this courageous adventure, *Annapurna*, is a great place to start.

This region was enclosed in the Annapurna Conservation Area Project (the ACAP), Nepal's first, in 1986, which contains over seven thousand, five hundred square kilometers. This was designated a 'conservation area' instead of a national park because of the sizeable populations residing in the numerous picturesque communities in this district. The ACAP administers the district and tries to engage the local people in a variety of programs to promote sanitation and sustainable tourism, reduce deforestation and erosion, and preserve local culture and traditions.

There is a great deal of geographical, linguistic, and cultural diversity within this extensive zone. At the lower altitudes, where the climate is quite lush and tropical, the trail passes through terraced fields of rice and groves of bananas and bamboo, with large tribes of langur monkeys chattering in the trees. The majority of the villagers living in these hot lower areas are Hindus. As you proceed upward into higher elevations, there is an extensive section of evergreen forest, and various Buddhist structures and traditions begin to mingle with the Hindu ones. Stupas and arched chortens, walls of mani stones, and rows of copper prayer wheels start to appear in these intermediate sections. And finally, in the highest landscapes above the timber line, the terrain becomes alpine and desert-like, and the cultural heritage, the religion, and the way of life are all very Tibetan.

The Annapurna Conservation Area Project also contains a number of popular, long-distance trekking routes. Two of the more well-known ones are the Annapurna Circuit and the Annapurna Sanctuary trek, which have long been considered to be some of the grandest walks in the world. The latter takes a highly scenic route through the center of the ACAP up to the Annapurna Base Camp, and the former makes a long, culturally rich circumnavigation of the entire Annapurna massif. The highest point on this route is the storied Thorung La Pass on the border of the Tibetan Plateau.

Until recently, most trekkers began the Annapurna Circuit in Besi Sahar, a bustling market town about an hour and a half's drive north from the mid-point of the Kathmandu–Pokhara highway. Most people normally walk the route counterclockwise from there over the pass to Jomsom, and then continue down to Pokhara via Poon Hill. This is the preferred direction because the elevation gains on the eastern side are more gradual, and because the section over Thorung La Pass from the western side is too long and too steep for most people to do comfortably in one day.

Most walkers going the whole way can generally complete the circuit in about three weeks, depending on how fast they walk and the number of rest days and side trips they want to fit into their schedule. However, in recent years there has been a considerable amount of road construction in the area. As a result of this, it is now possible to take local buses and four-wheel drives over much of the route, which greatly reduces the length of time required to make the full passage. The road is affecting the character and the popularity of the trail as well. A few decades ago, much of the Annapurna Circuit traversed remote, narrow paths that had an air of time travel to lost worlds. However, since the opening of the road, this is still a splendid walk, but it is not quite the same back-of-beyond experience that it was previously.

The time of year is another factor that greatly influences the nature of this trek. The main trekking season in Nepal is from October to December. At this time, the monsoon rains have passed, everything has been rinsed off and refreshed, the days are bright and sunny, and the views are at their grandest and clearest of the whole year. This is also by far the most crowded time. The lodges are jammed to capacity, the trails are full, there are long waits in the restaurants, and flights and bus rides can be difficult to arrange.

From the end of December until about the beginning of March, the Annapurna region is very cold, with temperatures during the night well below freezing. Trekking here in this season requires heavier loads with suitable warm clothing and proper sleeping bags. Also, much of the trail in the higher sections, especially over Thorung La Pass, is often blocked with deep snow and ice, and is unwalkable much of this time. In April and May, the snows have melted, the passes are open, the weather is usually sunny and unclouded, and the temperatures are a lot warmer. This is also the time of year when the rhododendrons, the fiery national flower of Nepal, ignite the hills in blazing reds and pinks. There are a lot more people on the trail in these months than there are during the winter, not surprisingly.

June to September is the time of the monsoon rains. The monsoon brings lots of cloudy days, reduced views, torrential downpours, and an increased danger of landslides. The mountain airstrips are often closed because of the cloudy weather, and there are a lot of flight cancellations. This is also the season when the notorious leeches appear. These can be very numerous and bothersome on some of the initial parts of the walk. However, despite these drawbacks, some people prefer this time of year because it is the lowest tourist season. There is hardly anyone walking these routes then, especially in June and July when the rains tend to be at their heaviest. Actually, the upper regions of the Annapurna Circuit are in the rain shadow of the Himalayas, so this area sees less rainfall than some of the sections below it, and many other parts of the country during these months. In addition, during the monsoon, the fields and the meadows are ablaze with broad swaths of delightful wild flowers. And another big plus is that you can walk with a small pack because it's not cold then. I for one really enjoy traveling in the Himalayas during the summer in spite of the monsoon. Just be sure to take along a supply of good books to read when the spectacular rains drive you indoors.

7

An adventure is only an inconvenience rightly considered;
An inconvenience is only an adventure wrongly considered.

G.K. Chesterton

A promising dawn was followed by a somewhat less than auspicious afternoon. Very early in the morning there was a pause in the overnight rains, which made getting across to the minibus station a much drier undertaking than it would have been otherwise. I left the hotel about four thirty a.m., which was just after closing time for most of the bars and discos in this touristy part of town. The street was full of revelers heading home in varying degrees of intoxication.

It was salutary, not to mention somewhat unusual, to see what drunkenness actually looks and sounds like from a position of sobriety. (I will never, ever do that again.) The taxi driver had promised to come at four forty-five, but I wasn't really expecting him to actually show up then, or even come at all. To my not inconsiderable surprise, he appeared on the very minute. Promptitude of this order is unheard of in these parts. I tipped him handsomely.

Minibuses in Nepal operate on a first come, first served basis, and they depart when they are full. The filling-up time usually lasts a while. What these drivers consider to be 'full' stretches credulity. They always think there is still room for one more passenger, even when there very clearly isn't. With a series of awkward contortions, I stuffed myself into the miniature seat, hunched over, knees jammed into the bench in front of me. When the driver noticed how awkwardly I filled the tight space, he thoughtfully suggested that I buy two seats and unfold. Five dollars to forestall seven hours of unbroken sardine syndrome would be money well spent, so I took him up on it. This was apparently the tipping point he had been looking for. We were now officially 'full', and soon away.

The most difficult part of a road journey in Nepal is getting out of town. The streets are choked with mighty conglomerations of snarled traffic that crawl along at a glacial pace, when they move at all. It takes a long time to cover the few kilometers from the center to the outskirts. This is a crowning opportunity to acquire merit by learning patience. In addition, much of the roadway is unpaved, resulting in blinkering levels of dust. The dust clouds engulfing our bus were so thick the driver had to switch on his brights to slog through them, even though we were now driving in full daylight. Seven hours and a whole lot of merit later, we eventually arrived in Besi Sahar, and gratefully disembarked.

Up until a few years ago, the bustling market town of Besi Sahar was the trailhead for the Annapurna Circuit. You started walking here, at the modest altitude of about eight hundred meters. These days, with the coming of the Manang Road, you have the option of continuing onward from Besi Sahar in local buses and shared jeeps. One of these jeeps was taking on passengers close to the minibus stop, and I got in. It was heading for the small village of Syange, about a three-to-four-hour ride farther up the mountain next to the Marsyangdi River. I selected this place because the route below it is often awash in mud and is not that attractive to walk on at this time of year. And beyond this village, the minimal track passes through an area of high, perpendicular cliffs I was not at all keen to negotiate by car. I am not as intrepid these days as I used to be. Syange seemed like a good place to start.

For about two hours or so all went well as we slowly bumped and splashed and lurched our way upwards. Then the jeep suddenly died on a very narrow stretch of the road, with a sheer wall on one side, and a steep drop overlooking the river on the other. We were stuck between the proverbial rock and a hard place, completely blocking any vehicles trying to come down from above us, or following along behind.

A traffic jam soon formed. As other vehicles arrived on the scene, their occupants got out, strolled over to our broken-down jeep, and stood around watching, giving opinions, and suggesting solutions. It had soon turned into quite the community project. For the next hour and a half, a succession of drivers and passengers took turns adjusting the hoses and the connections, energetically stoking up the battery, blowing out the fuel lines, cranking the ignition, and praying over the engine. While all this was going on, it was remarkable how relaxed, how cheerful, and how friendly everyone was. They were laughing and joking, and much amused by the whole thing. Nobody was complaining or stressed out, no one looked impatiently at a watch. No one tried to hustle the East here. This breakdown just wasn't a problem for these hardship-habituated mountain people at all. How calm and peaceful things can be where time is not money.

But despite all their goodwill and their combined efforts, the jeep refused to start. At this point the driver apologetically informed us that we would have to proceed to Syange on foot. While he was doing this, he refunded half the price of our fares, which I thought was a considerate and neighborly touch. We collected our various bags and bundles, and began walking up the miry track. As usual, the local people had soon left me trudging along way behind, straining under the unfamiliar load. A good way to discover just how out of shape you actually are is to put on a substantial backpack and start walking uphill in the Himalayas, shifting thirty-five pounds of extra body mass in addition to your pack weight. All that couch slugging catches up with you sooner or later.

I finally arrived at Syange just at dusk. This village is named for the sound of a sonorous waterfall nearby. Friendly residents ushered me into a simple and welcoming lodge right next to the heaving, rain-swollen river. Two French girls who were also walking the circuit were staying there as well. I was immediately impressed by how small their packs were. These were about the size of schoolchildren's book bags, and they only weighed about four kilos. Even after all the culling and sorting and dumping I had just done back in Kathmandu, my pack was still at least three or four times as heavy. How do these ultra-light folks do it? Sipping some evening tea with them in the dining room, I silently vowed to take up their unencumbered style henceforth.

The rains began drumming on the tin roof a short while later, mixing nicely with the rush of the Marsyangdi just outside. All this water music was very soothing after the crowds, the smog, and the noise of the capital, followed by the discomforts of a long, cramped day on the road. I opened the window, stretched out on the minimal bed, and luxuriated in the rich sounds off and on through the night.

I do enjoy knocking around in Kathmandu, but I was happy to be out of it now. The cities of the Subcontinent heave and teem like cities almost nowhere else. The smothering press of their relentless flows of people can be oppressive, sometimes even frightening. I think Calcutta (Kolkata) is probably the hands-down front runner in this department, but there are a number of other cities that are not far behind, such as Old Delhi. To describe Old Delhi as 'a bit on the crowded side' would be a significant understatement.

I once stayed there for a few days with the same son mentioned in the Tamil Nadu adventure earlier. One evening just after dark we were making our way back to the hotel through some thickly packed streets after a day of poking around in the fascinating bazaars of the old town. We were walking along one of the wider avenues in the Chandni Chowk (Moonlight Square) area near the Red Fort. The street was very dimly lit, and it was filled with solid masses of people from curb to curb for hundreds of meters. Suddenly a motor rickshaw erupted from the crowd right in front of us. We both immediately dodged out of the way towards either side of it. It was gone in an instant, swallowed up by the sea of humanity all around us. And so was my small son. He had completely vanished into the dense crush and the darkness.

This was the stuff of heart attacks. Frantically I groped around in the slowly shifting walls of bodies for about twenty minutes, but there was no sign of him anywhere. Then, filled with the most drastic visions of the worst possible outcomes, I stumbled back towards the small hotel, thoroughly shocked and deeply miserable, in full-on panic mode. I had just lost a young child in a vast, dangerous city at night. What should I do now? Where could I go for help? What would I tell his mother, who had pleaded with me not to bring him? What happens to children who get lost in India? This was a truly horrific moment, one of the worst of my life. At this point, I was completely at a loss about how to proceed.

But, as I approached the narrow entrance to the hotel in absolute confusion and devastation, there he was, waiting patiently on the front steps, tinkering with his Swiss Army knife. He was just old enough to understand what he needed to do in this situation, and to find his way back to the hotel through the darkness and the massive crowds on his own. I just about toppled over on the spot. Flooded with relief, I bungled up the stairs to the room and collapsed onto the balcony, where I poured myself a very robust Scotch, hands a-tremble. I sat out there for a long time, slowly coming down from the adrenaline, and still imagining the awful scenarios that might have been. As only Mark Twain could put it:

> I am an old man, and I have had many troubles, most of which never even happened.

8

*Crossing the summer river,
sandals in my hand.*

Buson

In the Himalayas it is very important to make your way up into the high country slowly. A useful rule of thumb is to limit your ascent to about five hundred meters a day for the first ten days. Having just come from a life right at sea level, this precaution was especially appropriate now. Syange is situated at an elevation of about eleven hundred meters. This would make the scenic village of Tal, located at around seventeen hundred meters, the upper limit for the day. On my legs, Tal was going to be roughly a six-or-seven-hour walk.

The trail between them passes through one of the most beautiful and dangerous sections on the Annapurna Circuit. This is a region of cascading streams launching themselves over perilous drop-offs. Here the path traverses an expanse of spectacular, vertical cliffs and sheer, towering rock faces, festooned with numerous, gauze-like ribbons of water plummeting almost a kilometer from the heights above to the floor of the Marsyangdi gorge. In summer, everything is luxuriantly green from all the rains. On this section, the jeep drivers proceed very slowly and carefully: a mishap here, and it's all over. These mountain drivers are very skillful at what they do, and they rarely come to grief, but it does happen betimes. On the day before this one, we passed the battered remains of a jeep that had taken such a plunge, killing all of its occupants. I was glad to be on foot.

As I walked cautiously along next to the steep cliffs, I was trying out a new walking stick I had found in a small shop on a side street on the way out. I usually like to carry walking sticks that are about five feet long. That seems to be the best overall length for negotiating steep descents and precipitous stream crossings on wobbly stepping stones. This staff was a bit shorter than my usual ones, but it was sturdy and nicely turned, and it had felt comfortable in the shop. It also seemed to impress the growling village dogs I was encountering along the way.

Dogs in this region know a great deal about sticks. They have a lot of experience with them. Another time in Old Delhi, I was sitting on the balcony of my hotel people-watching a few hours before dinner time. As I surveyed the comings and goings below, two policemen strolled past on the other side of the street carrying lathis. Lathis are five-foot lengths of stout bamboo tipped with sturdy brass fittings at either end. These heavy sticks are mainly designed for crowd control, but they have other uses as well.

As they passed by opposite my balcony, a nasty, rather mangy-looking street dog approached them, snarling and menacing. One of the policemen quickly dropped back a few paces, concealed himself behind a parked van, and raised his formidable staff over his head. The other officer, pretending to be afraid, backpedaled away from the dog past his unseen partner. The dog instantly went after him, and as it charged by the van, the officer hiding there slammed the lathi down on its back full force.

What a howl. I had never seen an animal take such a lethal blow. The dog crumpled into a heap on the street, shaking and twitching, and I was thinking that was probably the end of it. However, after a while, it somehow managed to rise and drag itself off and hide under another car nearby. With educations like that, these hapless creatures really do know just about all there is to know about sticks. When a vicious dog threatens you hereabouts, all you usually have to do is strike your stick smartly on a rock or the pavement, and it will desist. This is especially effective if your stick has a good, thick section of iron pipe mounted on the end, as mine did.

As I continued upwards towards Tal, the dogs kept their distance, but it was not long before I was bitten by my first leech. Leeches are a major seasonal hazard during monsoon time. These are not the finger-length, black leeches often featured in jungle disaster movies, like the ones that beset Humphrey Bogart in *The African Queen*. The leeches that infest these foothill areas are the small, brown ones that are about an inch or so long when they are empty.

This bite occurred during an especially boisterous stream crossing. This stream was a bit too deep and rampant to attempt while wearing boots, so I had to sit down on the side of the path to take them off before wading across in bare feet. And then I had to do this again when I got to the other side to put them back on. Somewhere in there, either while I was sitting on the grass, or as I reached down to pick up my pack and the stick afterwards, this leech had attached itself to my hand, hidden between my thumb and forefinger. I didn't notice it until sometime later when I happened to look down and saw my hand bleeding copiously. I squashed it off, and cleaned up the mess as best I could with a handful of tissues. This bleeding continued for some time: These leeches inject you with a chemical that prevents coagulation and increases blood flow. They also implant an anesthetic so you don't feel their bite. Crafty little buggers, these.

Leeches can attach themselves to you in various ways. They can drop onto you from overhanging vegetation, or climb onto your shoes from ground level. They can also catch on as you brush past them on rocks and bushes on the side of the trail. I had heard that applying a range of caustic liquids to your boots and socks can help keep them at bay, things like lemon juice, eucalyptus oil, dish soap, kerosene, and cheap cologne. Liberal applications of table salt are said to be effective as well. Having none of the above, I had to soldier on as best I could.

Farther on, another leech somehow managed to get onto the back of my other hand. This one had not actually broken the skin yet. It was just fixing to bite me when I discovered it. When I tried to pluck it off, I was surprised by the strength and the tenacity of its grip. As small as it was, and even though it wasn't even attached with its jaws, this tiny creature was absolutely set on staying right where it was.

Leech number three appeared at a tea stall while I was taking a break about midday. Concerned about getting blisters, I had taken off my boots to dry my stream-soaked feet, and discovered this one feasting away right through one of the socks. I pulled it off and tossed it on the ground about two meters away. Undeterred, and not in the least taking *no* for an answer, it immediately started crawling right back towards me. I marveled at its focus and dedication. However, by that point, this resolute, unwavering determination to make a meal of me was getting on my nerves. I picked up a boot and whacked it, leaving a vivid splotch of my own blood on the stones.

When I arrived at my destination later that afternoon, I went to my room to change into dry clothes. As I did this, I found some other small holes in the ankle region bleeding steadily. Apparently, the anti-coagulant keeps on working for some hours after the leech itself has dropped off. I swabbed away with alcohol wipes and iodine, and covered the holes with lots of tape. It looked like there was no real harm done, unless of course these things carried some exotic, long-term disease I didn't know about. I had hoped that the previous night's deluge would have washed these unpleasant fellows away, but this was clearly not the case. Fortunately, there is a leech line, an altitude level beyond which the leeches don't go. Once you get above about two and a half thousand meters, the leech problem disappears, but today I had been right in the middle of their zone.

9

The bridegroom's doors are open wide,
And I am next of kin;
The guests are met, the feast is set:
May'st hear the merry din.

Samuel Taylor Coleridge

The village of Tal sits on a large bend in the Marsyangdi River. This is where it gets its name: *Tal* means lake. The bend is so wide it looks like a lake, and it makes this village one of the most attractive and restful places in the Annapurna region. It actually was a lake for a while a long time ago when a landslide blocked the course of the river here. It even has a sandy beach, although not very many people try to go swimming in the icy meltwaters coming down from the snows above. There are also a number of large, thumping waterfalls pouring from the cliffs close by. Tal does not have a water problem. This village marks the start of the Manang district.

The path beyond Tal was on the old Annapurna Circuit cut right into the cliffs overhanging the river. This part of the trail has become much cleaner and greener since the coming of the road. Before the road went in, this entire area was supplied by frequent horse trains dressed up in red head plumes and brass bells fastened around their necks on brightly dyed woolen belts. These bells made a pleasant and melodious jingling as the horses approached you along the trail, like a traveling wind chime. Far less pleasant were the pools of urine and the piles of horse dung they left along the path. All that is now gone. These horse trains have been replaced by the jeeps, and this rugged section of the trail had been thoroughly washed and renewed by the rains.

A few hours later, there was a fork in the path at Dharapani, a large village where two main rivers come together. It is well named. *Dharapani* means 'place of flowing water'. From here, the Annapurna Circuit continues along the Marsyangdi gorge up towards the left, and another path going over the high Larka La Pass into the Manaslu region ascends the narrow valley of the Dudh Khola off to the right. (See the map in chapter 6.) Naming things after prominent water features does seem to be something of a trend around here.

There is no road over to the Manaslu side from here, so that area is still supplied by horse and mule caravans, which wait in Dharapani for loads coming up from Besi Sahar by jeep. As a result, much of this village is still littered with horse manure, which attracts clouds of insects and generates some rather pungent odors. When I arrived, I considered stopping here because the darkening skies were clearly preparing a hard rain. But when I went exploring to look for a suitable lodge, the bugs and the aromas changed my mind. I decided to push on for another hour or so. As I was heading out of the village, a friendly baby goat appeared, and walked along with me for several kilometers. It seemed to think I was going somewhere it needed to be. I thought perhaps the walking stick I was carrying had led it to confuse me with its regular shepherd. A very cute and cheering little companion indeed.

Just before the cloudburst that had been threatening for some time began in earnest, I came to the village of Donakyu. This was a smaller, much cleaner, and far more appealing place than Dharapani. Not only was this village dung-free, it also had numerous apple and plum orchards loaded with ripening fruit, and thriving flower gardens around traditional, chalet-like homes. Clusters of *namaste*-chanting children played in the street while easygoing villagers tended to their vegetable patches and repaired their structures and walls. My lodge was one of the most attractive ones I found anywhere along the trail, with high, wooden balconies overhanging a paved courtyard abundantly planted with red and pink roses. As the rain hammered on the roof, I holed up under the sleeping bag in my basic but homey room, suffused with a feeling of well-being and tranquility.

What a difference just a few kilometers can make. And this is not infrequently the case here in the Subcontinent, I have discovered. A few years before this, I had been traveling in the foothills north of Delhi. At one point, I needed to cross over to the railway grid a bit to the south of me, but there was no convenient way to do this. Another day's ride on a long-distance, government bus was unavoidable. As with the other bus trip I described previously, I was looking at a jarring, dawn-to-dusk noise-fest, in thick, funereal traffic, crimped into a miniature seat with no leg room, with half of the passengers standing up in the aisles leaning over those sitting down, and so forth. It was this ride that produced the *don't get on the bus to spare life or limb* doctrine that I religiously adhere to today. I got on the bus at sunrise, and when I finally lurched off of that thing at sundown, I was a nervous wreck, desperately in need of a stiff drink.

However, the district I had landed in did not look very conducive to unwinding and relaxing at all. Even though I was now back on the railroad network, this place was pretty rough. It was a scene of smoke-belching trucks, unfinished buildings, dense crowds, rusting billboards, brawling dogs, noisy machinery, garbage-choked 'streams', and dingy plastic-on-cardboard shanties on all sides. For the beleaguered people who were living there, this was truly a hard station. It was one of the more difficult and stressful arrivals I have done, and after such a long day of grueling travel, I was not coping with it all that graciously. I walked straight to the nearest hotel that looked halfway operational, and went to bed, vowing to be gone on the first train out I could find.

Accordingly, bright and early the next morning, I was sitting in the breakfast room having some coffee and planning my escape on the map. While I was doing this, two tourists from Norway came in and sat down at a table nearby, and we exchanged the usual sort of greetings and travelers' pleasantries common to such occasions. As it turned out, they had just come from another town a few kilometers down the road called Vrindavan, and they could not say enough in praise of it. They positively raved about the place, insisting that it was absolutely a must-see. Their recommendation changed my plans. Instead of getting on the train, I decided to postpone my departure and go see this wonder. I seriously doubted that something meriting such a glowing report could exist anywhere near the discouraging views unfolding outside the hotel. Nevertheless, after breakfast I collected my bags and searched out a rickshaw driver willing to take me there. And was I glad that I did. The Norwegians' description was spot on. Vrindavan turned out to be one of the most fascinating and colorful towns I have ever seen.

Vrindavan is a very old city on the banks of the Yamuna River south of Delhi. For long ages it has been a site of pilgrimage, drawing spiritual wanderers from far and near. Itinerant, wide-ranging holy men and women overwinter there, camping out on string beds by the river, waiting for the snows on the high passes of the northern pilgrim routes to melt. This town is well provided with historic temples and ancient shrines. It is also home to a number of traditional dharmsalas, rudimentary dormitories for pilgrims that cost almost nothing. These are enclosed courtyards with rows of tiny sleeping cells along the sides, and a small fountain for drinking, ablutions, and foot-washing in the middle. The cells don't have doors. There is only a basic chain-link grate to keep out the thieving monkeys that live on the roof.

A kindly, English-speaking citizen befriended me as I strolled into town from the rickshaw stand. He suggested that I stay in one of these dharmsalas, and led me through a confusing warren of back alleys and side streets to the gates of a venerable, Moghul Era building fronted by a wide, pointed archway. In the entry hall a few paces beyond this arch, there was a massive, well-worn rosewood desk, at which sat an equally massive registrar somewhere in the three-to-four-hundred-pound range. This ponderous official was attired in a white lunghi and a long, white pajama top, an ample, multi-stranded turban, a large streak of bright orange paint on his forehead, and a thicket of impressive, Blackbeard-esque facial hair.

Sitting on the desk just in front of him there was an over-sized, leather-bound ledger with pages that were almost a yard wide. These pages had been neatly ruled into several dozen long, narrow columns for recording the most intricate and detailed information I have ever been asked to provide: name, point of origin, caste, profession, annual salary, method of travel to Vrindavan, proposed means of travel home, father's name, mother's name, father's profession, god of preference, reason for coming, intended length of current stay, dietary restrictions, age, hair color, height, weight, hat size, and so on.

When this extensive round of data entry was completed, I was invited to select a cell in the adjoining courtyard. This tiny room was very simple: an eight-by-five-foot closet with a thin, foam mattress on a rough, flagstone floor. There were no locks, no numbers, no coat hooks, no nothing except the gentle splashing of the sweet little fountain close by. There were also some large drifts of fresh flowers several meters deep left by other pilgrims piled up along one of the courtyard walls. I walked over there and collected a generous headscarf-full and strewed them across the floor of my cell to get into the proper mood of the thing. I was delighted. Real India at last! I dropped my bag on the stones and headed out to see the town.

This dharmsala was close to the river, and I soon found myself approaching the water. On the beach in front of me there was an aged, heavily patched canvas tent, with a long, crooked pole standing next to it. On the top of this pole there was a cheap, rusty loudspeaker emitting a soft, squeaky voice plaintively chanting a mantra over and over. The phrase gently droning from the speaker was: *Hare Om Namah Shivaya,* one of the oldest and most beloved of Indian mantras. The small woman inside the tent was quite famous. Some bystanders told me that she had been sitting in that tent repeating this mantra continuously by day and by night for over forty years, with only a few hours' sleep per day. She was held in great esteem by the townspeople and village folks nearby. Dozens of these well-wishers came and sat quietly on the sand outside of her tent, listening reverently.

In addition, because Vrindavan was also a center for the Hare Krishna Movement, the streets of the town were full of Hare Krishna adherents from all over the country and from many foreign lands as well. The devotees from in-country were notably cheerful and relaxed. They were clearly having a wonderful time. They were singing, they were chanting, celebrating, worshiping, and rejoicing, as happy as clams at high tide. There were a large number of devotees from North American and Western European countries as well, both men and women. Most of this foreign contingent appeared to be middle-aged folks with very short haircuts and stern expressions. These folks didn't appear to be celebrating and rejoicing quite as much as the natives, however. They were conducting themselves in a rather different spirit than the Indian disciples. For them, the pilgrimage to Vrindavan was serious business. This tends to happen fairly often in the East when it comes to some of these spiritual things. The Westerners just don't seem to get it in the same way that the locals do.

Another major attraction of the town was the daily public lunch provided in a ballroom-sized hall in the palatial Hare Krishna Temple about midday. At the appointed time, lines of pilgrims and travelers holding their ten-rupee meal tickets filed in to the hall and sat down in long rows on plastic beach mats neatly arranged across the floor. When everyone was seated, a small army of servers in orange robes walked along in front of them distributing various components of the menu. First came the dish-wallahs, handing out green plates made of oval-shaped leaves neatly toothpicked together. After them came the rice dispensers, who shoveled spoonfuls of white rice on to the plates from large stainless-steel buckets. This team was followed by another wave of attendants who doled out portions of lentil stew, vegetable curry, boiled spinach, and red pepper sauce next to the rice as they passed down the aisles.

The food was wonderful. It was beautifully cooked and cheerfully served, and almost free (around twenty-five cents). In addition, it was completely clean and safe to eat. You would not get the runs here. We stuffed ourselves without restraint, me using a spoon I had specially picked up in the bazaar for the occasion. (I never quite got the eating rice and curry with your hands thing.) It was one of the best meals I had ever had in all of India. A big thank you to the hosts, and to the Norwegian travelers who recommended Vrindavan back there in the breakfast room.

This scene reminds me of another temple feast that happened about a day's train ride to the northwest. This one was laid on in the Golden Temple of Amritsar, revered by the Sikhs. The Golden Temple is also a very old and famous place of worship, and thousands of pilgrims and travelers come great distances to visit it. The daily public lunch served here was another large-scale function similar to the one at the Hare Krishna Temple in Vrindavan. This one also took place in a very large hall, with row upon row of diners sitting on the floor, leaf plates dispensed en masse, and a corps of rice, dhal, and curry servers ladling their way along the lines of guests. However, what truly made this operation especially memorable was the grand kitchen where all of this bountiful hospitality originated. It was magnificent, something Gulliver might have seen in Brobdingnag.

This kitchen was in a large room behind the dining hall. It was approximately the dimensions of a badminton court, with high ceilings and tall, narrow windows. Along one wall there were massive cauldrons of rice, big enough to boil a camel in, bubbling away. These were attended by groups of lunghi-clad kitchen workers plying spoons the size of canoe paddles with both hands. Along a second wall there was another row of these prodigious tubs full of simmering dhal. At this station, assorted spices like red pepper, turmeric, and cumin were being stirred in by the bucketful.

But the most striking scene of all was the chapati production line happening in the middle of the room. In the center of the kitchen, there was a heavy-duty brass tray the size of a ping-pong table containing an enormous blob of chapati dough about as big as a small car. Lord knows how they ever got it in there. I didn't see that part. Sitting on the floor on two sides of this flour mountain there was a line of apron-clad ladies rapidly slicing off handfuls of dough, shaping them into balls about the size of tangerines, and then scooting them across the floor to another row of ladies with rolling pins and small round bread boards. With two or three deft strokes, these rolling-pin ladies expanded the dough balls into chapatis, and then, without looking, tossed them backwards over their shoulders onto a colossal, upside-down wok about six feet behind them. Let me repeat that: *without even looking*.

This wok was on the same scale as the rest of the place. It was at least five feet across, and made from black cast iron about half an inch thick. They must have needed a forklift to shift it. It was placed upside down over a large gas burner similar to the ones used for cooking paella in Spain. After the rolling-pin ladies had tossed the chapatis on to this super-heated wok, they were supervised by a crew of baking meisters perched on shelves above it, equipped with long metal rods. When these fellows decided that a chapati was properly done, they speared it with one of their rods and neatly flicked it across the kitchen Frisbee-style into a line of capacious wicker baskets standing about twelve feet away. I never saw them miss, not once.

All this highly synchronized activity never stopped. Picture if you will dozens of dough balls rolling swiftly across the floor, spreading out into chapatis, lofting gracefully up on to the wok, gliding through the air into the baskets, and then being carried away to the dining hall in one smooth, continuous flow. It was like from something from *Fantasia* or one of those fine, old, musical cartoons from the 1940s with singing plates and cutlery. The only thing missing was the soundtrack. These people were truly experts at what they were doing, and it was a joy to watch.

10

Smultronställe (noun);
'Place of wild strawberries';
A cherished location where you find
comfort, renewal and peace.

Swedish word

I woke up the next morning to a cold, drizzling fog. This didn't feel like summer at all. I thought of just staying put in my comfortable room in the rose garden and taking a rest day, but after drinking some coffee I decided to carry on. Nothing like a little caffeine to rev up the spirit of adventure.

However, after two hours of steep ascent through a

dripping, misty forest, past several crashing waterfalls throwing sheets of spray over the trail, my clothes were wet through, and I was rapidly becoming chilled. A more determined sprinkling soon brought out the green plaid umbrella I had acquired from a street vendor down in Besi Sahar. This deflected most of the rain effectively, but I was still getting wetter and colder from the fog. It occurred to me that continuing up into increasing altitude under these conditions for several more hours might well be a formula for hypothermia, especially if the usual afternoon wind set in. When I came to the small settlement of Timang a short while later, I decided it would probably be best to stop there.

Even though it was only about ten a.m., I checked into a suitable guest house, put on dry clothes, and climbed into my sleeping bag. I was very glad that this had not been left behind in the luggage room back in Kathmandu, as it almost was. You can take the ultra-light thing too far, especially in the Himalayas. However, a highly likely candidate for the luggage rooms of the future will be my wonderfully comfortable XL cotton T-shirt. This is by far the most pleasant walking garment I have, but in monsoon conditions it simply will not dry out, even when it's hung up in a breeze for a whole day. Because there is so much moisture in the air during this season, the cotton just keeps on absorbing more and more water, even inside a hotel room.

By mid-afternoon the rains and the mists were still going strong, and the wind was indeed picking up, as I had feared. Even though I had not made much progress, getting off the trail early had been the right thing to do. I spent the remains of the day resting and reading in bed. The dreary conditions settling in outside reminded me of another time of wayfaring house arrest, and the ghosts of travels past were soon astir in that snug little room on the second floor.

The first time I was adrift on the road came early in my college career. Two or three months into my sophomore year, I found myself unable to go on. I didn't know what to do with college at that time. I decided to take a break and think things over. I left the university, and started hitch-hiking across America as the first snows of the year were falling on I-90 in Boston. Standing out there in the slush, I had hardly any idea about where I was going other than *West*, and no plans for what I was going to do when I got there. I was a deeply confused young person at this point.

Fortunately, there are some really generous and helpful people cruising the highways of the US of A. The drivers I met out there were very nice to me. About three weeks, a good many rides, and a large measure of the kindness of strangers later, I caught a late flight from San Francisco to Maui, and deposited myself on the beach behind the airport. At this stage, I was not sufficiently prepared for the deep North American winter now hitting its full stride back on the mainland to do anything else. A few days later, I went out exploring, and after a few weeks, I eventually came across an inviting cave at the bottom of a tall cliff in a remote part of the island. And, much in need of protection from the seasonal rains, I moved in.

This cave had many virtues. It was quite spacious. The ceilings were high enough to stand upright and walk around under. It was deep, and it was dry. It was right next to the water, almost in it, in fact. Little waves ricocheted off of some large rocks nearby and glided gently into the lower part of it, which was very convenient for keeping clean and washing up. In addition, this place was free. And, most critically, there was an extensive, richly stockpiled dump cascading down the cliff about half a mile away. This dump was vital because moving into a slanting, rocky cave hard by the ocean entails several essential steps:

Step 1. Go down to the dump and round up a substantial stack of long, sturdy boards.

Step 2. Haul these boards over to the cave and arrange them into a stable and reasonably level platform. Return to the dump and get additional boards to reinforce this structure as necessary.

Step 3. When this basic platform has been consolidated, go back to the dump and cast about until you find an appealing carpet that is about the same size as your platform. Drag the carpet back to the cave, rinse it thoroughly in the ocean, and then drape it across some convenient rocks and dry it in the sun. This may take two or three days, and even longer if it is raining. Not to worry. The rain will wash away any salt left over from the rinsing operation.

Step 4. Once the carpet has dried, install it on the platform and smooth it out. It might also be a good idea to place some suitable flat rocks on the corners to hold it down, depending on your esthetic sense. At this point you have an inhabitable cave, and you can take up residence in basic, if not especially lavish comfort.

This is more or less the minimum decor required to preserve decency in this sort of living arrangement.

However, you need not stop there. There was a fellow traveler living in another cave a few hundred meters down the beach who had been there for several years. He had not stopped at this basic platform stage by any means. Over time he had also acquired a comfortable armchair, a book shelf, a library, and a large cabinet filled with a varied array of dishes, pots, glasses, storage jars, coffee mugs, cooking utensils, and cutlery, all gleaned from this same cornucopian dump. Cave dwelling in the grand manner, as it were. Therefore, when you move into your next cave, you need not be overly minimalist in your approach. Get on down to your neighborhood dump and rummage and gather and furnish at will, according to your personal inclinations.

I had discovered this cave during the height of the rainy season. Even though it was roomy and well protected from the showers, it was also very remote and isolated. One afternoon, after almost a week of drizzling days, I was starting to get depressed. The overcast skies, the continuous dampness outside, and the loneliness were getting to me. Also, I had been reading a rather gloomy novel that I picked up in the dump. This was a battered copy of Fyodor Dostoyevsky's *The Possessed*. This old book wasn't helping my spirits very much either. But then in the evening, the rain stopped, a thin strip of clear sky opened on the horizon, and a burst of warm, red light flooded into the cave. Feeling pretty loony by then, I decided that it would be healthy to seize this opportunity and pop across to my neighbor's cave for some much-needed human contact. A round of tea and conversation was in order. I emerged from my lonesome refuge and made my way along the bottom of the cliff over to his place.

However, I was not at all prepared for what I found there. My laid back, cheerful neighbor was not at home. Instead, at the entrance of his cave, tinged in deep red by the setting sun, there stood a huge stranger almost seven feet tall, wearing only a pair of ragged Levi's. He uttered a gruff hello in an unusually deep and intimidating voice, like something Lurch in *The Addams Family* might have said when he answered the door. This was not the calming social therapy I had anticipated at all.

There was something really odd about this individual. It took me a while to grasp what it was. Suddenly it hit me: his head was completely shaved, everywhere. And I don't mean just his hair and his beard. He had removed all of his eyebrows as well. As you know, clean shaven faces abound all over the world, and smoothly shaved heads are highly fashionable everywhere. But when you combine the effects of absolutely no hair and no eyebrows at all with this person's extreme size, the dramatic setting, the crimson sunset, and the ominous voice, you find yourself in a real spook-house moment. Thoroughly unnerved by all this, I quickly mumbled a scant, confused explanation about looking for my neighbor, and then scurried back along the rocky shore in the gloaming.

Early the next morning, I woke up with the overwhelming inclination to get away from there as soon as possible. I had been sitting alone in the rain for too long, and the previous evening's encounter with the hairless giant had pushed me over the edge. It was time for a change of scene. I quickly grabbed the basics, and set out on an extensive tour of Maui, following the shoreline on foot. This expedition took me through a wide range of different areas and terrains: across arid savannahs and along remote beaches, into lush, flowering rain forests, and up steep volcanos on black, ankle-wrenching lava flows, with long views of the ocean far below.

This hastily arranged jaunt turned into a much more robust and involved undertaking than I had anticipated. Physically it proved to be far more demanding than I expected. Mentally it became something of a rite of passage. I was strangely preoccupied, often just drifting along on auto-pilot. My journal is dotted with dreamy reflections and a number of introspective poems that I composed aloud as I walked.

> Lines on the beach where waves had gone no
>   further;
> Marks of drops of water splashed on the sand;
> Footprints of a giant bird;
> Footsteps of me.

And the like, verging on the incoherent.

After several weeks, this energetic circumnavigation eventually brought me back around the island to my modest shelter. As beautiful and as catalytic as all this varied landscape had been, I was glad to be back. After this long spell of sleeping on the ground out in the open, and tiring of the mental gymnastics, I was really looking forward to being at 'home', and just blobbing out by the water. However, a few days before I got there, the highly celebrated Hawaiian winter surf had arrived on the shore where the cave was. For almost a week, thirty-foot waves a mile long and about three hundred yards apart slammed relentlessly into the cliff. I sat at the top of it and watched them for hours.

These waves were truly impressive, with long trains of spray streaming from their crests as they broke into the wind with a thundering, crashing roar. I had often been on beaches in Africa in near hurricane conditions, but I had never seen anything like this.

After a few days, when the huge waves had diminished a bit, we beachcombers climbed down the cliff to see how our caves had fared. As we were now fully expecting, these comfortable little retreats had been completely washed out. The laboriously constructed platforms, the neat carpets, the driftwood, the extra clothes, the water jars, the brown rice, the cutlery, the books, and the furniture were nowhere to be seen. There was nothing left. As the Buddhists so nicely render it: *Impermanence is swift.*

11

*Many will be rudely shocked
by those that they find in Heaven.*

John Newton (attributed)

As a result of this rather dramatic washout, us cave dwellers were now homeless once again. Over the next week or so, we shifted ourselves to the outlying beach areas and the public parks around Lahaina, the old whaling port on the south side of the island. One sunny morning, I sat on a bench airing and sorting the water-logged contents of my pack on the grass. While I was sitting there, up strolled the same huge person I had last seen in my neighbor's cave a few weeks before the great waves appeared. This time, in the broad light of day, he didn't seem quite as spooky to me as he had back there in the twilight. We quickly got into a fellow-refugee sort of conversation, and to my surprise, we started to hit it off rather well. As Franz Kafka once wrote:

> First impressions are always unreliable.

On this occasion, he exhibited a much gentler aspect than he had the first time. During my last few months at college, I had been taking a class in comparative religious literature, exploring the central themes of the world's major faiths. Before I hitch-hiked away, I had taken the textbook for the course, and cut out some of the passages that appealed to me. I stuffed them into a notebook in a side pocket and forgot about them. Somehow these pages had survived the pounding of the waves that wrecked my cave. I discovered them afterwards, floating in a tide pool nearby. They were now sitting in a soggy jumble on the park bench among some of my other stuff. My visitor picked them up and carefully smoothed them out to dry in the sun.

You're going to need these, he said quietly.

Out on the street, my unexpected new

acquaintance had been nicknamed 'Peter the Giant'. And, as you may have already inferred, Peter the Giant had a rather interesting story: One does not usually get to the eyebrow-shaving stage overnight. He had been a seaman of the Merchant Marine in the Pacific Ocean for a number of years, indulging heartily in all things that type of life affords. One evening, as he was standing watch in the prow of his ship far out at sea, he experienced a powerful epiphany of some kind. He described it as an overpowering, dazzling light falling on him suddenly, something along the road-to-Damascus lines. And, it turned out, he was not alone in this. He found out later that his girlfriend, who was then many thousands of miles away, experienced something similar at the same time. However, he didn't go into a lot of detail about this event, so I'm not exactly sure what happened to him out there. Putting it in the vernacular, he got zapped.

After such a sudden and mind-blowing development, he decided that he needed some down time to digest all this. He jumped ship in Hawaii soon afterwards, and headed up into the hills for a season of reflection and meditation. When he came down, he was a changed man, he had reinvented himself. He now had a conspicuous aura about him that was noticeable from a distance. He radiated a strange, ethereal glow that unsettled many of the people who encountered him. He also had no money. All he owned was that pair of old Levi's and a tattered army surplus sleeping bag, and he went about barefooted and bare-chested. I think the eyebrow-shaving thing had started about then.

It was not just his unusual appearance that was alarming. His wavelength, and his behavior, deeply unnerved a lot of people as well. One day I bumped into him on my way to do some laundry, so I invited him to come along. He stood in the laundromat in bare feet, wearing his old sleeping bag like a sarong while his jeans went through the wash. He wasn't saying anything, but his unusual persona was making the other laundromat patrons noticeably uncomfortable. They didn't know what to think of this guy. When our clothes were washed and dried, I suggested going to a nearby supermarket to pick up something to eat. As we arrived at the store, he announced: *I know what I want. I want raw hamburger*, and he wandered off in search of that. A few minutes later he came back and told me that raw hamburger was not available. Switching to Plan B, he said: *I'll get cookies*, and he walked away to look for those. He returned shortly, holding a foot-long cylinder of some biscuits he fancied. Not waiting until we were back outside, he deftly snapped the cylinder in the middle and handed half of it to me, in a very spontaneous and open-hearted sort of way. He started eating these cookies right there on the spot, as if it were totally ordinary to feed yourself standing in a supermarket aisle, half-dressed and in bare feet, without bothering to visit the cashier.

Somewhere around this time, we heard about a spiritual center on the other side of the island, and a couple of us beach hippies went over there to visit it. We arrived just as this community was preparing for a lunch out on the porch. They kindly invited us to join them, which we did. However, all of their gracious hospitality notwithstanding, almost immediately we began to sense that there was something strange about this place. It felt like we had stepped into an elaborate rehearsal of some sort, an odd scene of refined make-believe. The guiding inspiration there seemed to be *let's play sages of the bamboo grove.*

They had definitely assembled all the right props. Even keen-eyed Hergé himself (the widely traveled creator of Tintin) would have been hard put to arrange all the details of this stage set with more precision and thoroughness than they had achieved here. Out in the garden, a blossoming tree dropped cream-colored petals onto the lawn at suitable intervals, sonorous wind chimes swayed in the breeze, and pinkish lotus flowers brightened up a central goldfish pond. The main building was a breezy, cavernously empty assembly hall with wide teak floorboards and thick, heavy beams set into white walls. On the veranda in front of this, there was a long, low dining table laid out with tasteful stoneware and highly polished wooden bowls, enameled chopsticks, and graceful, hand-carved serving utensils. The residents gathered around this table on the floor, sitting on their knees in the Japanese style, and conducted the healthful vegetarian luncheon with a discreetly orchestrated 'simplicity' reminiscent of a tea ceremony.

After lunch, we were invited to step into the hall for a personal consultation with 'The Master'. One of the people sitting at the table had told me that up until his retirement several years previously, this gentleman had been a coat-and-tie, mid-management joe back in LA. Now, more in keeping with his new incarnation as a 'wise one', he was arrayed in bare feet, a pair of black, calf-length, cotton trousers with a drawstring, a loose-fitting tunic made of the same material, a wispy gray goatee, and an amulet symbolizing infinity suspended around his neck. And nicely offsetting this studied ensemble, he had also taken on a soft-spoken, slightly foreign-sounding accent that omitted words like *a* and *the* and plurals in strategic places. We took up the formal Japanese sitting position on the wooden floor, and were edified with a well-meant discourse on the cardinal points of spiritual progress, garnished with pithy insights of the *every road leads in two directions* variety. As this meeting ended, their afternoon session was getting underway, so we thanked them for the lunch and the visit, and returned to the Lahaina side of the island.

Back on the beach, I started a fire and put the kettle on, as was my wont. While I was adjusting the wood and nursing the water along to a proper boil, my giant, tea-loving associate came over and planted himself on the sand. When I told him about the day's excursion, his reaction was as unvarnished as it was brief. He said: *Heaven thinks about as much of fake sages as it does of LSD.* Which might not have been all that wide of the mark, actually.

One Sunday morning soon afterwards, Peter the Giant went out to a large, opulent church that had a copper roof and an acre of expensive foreign cars sitting outside. He took off all of his clothes in the parking lot, and then walked down the central aisle of the church stark naked in the middle of the service, declaiming on divine expectations, describing judgements to come, and so forth. The result is not hard to imagine. Rich people just aren't used to this sort of thing. Nobody is used to this sort of thing. That congregation was thoroughly startled.

As a result of activities like these, most of the people in the town were very uneasy around him. He was just too far beyond their comfort zone. For some reason, I didn't find him all that alarming. I had been brewing afternoon tea with him on the beach almost daily ever since the cave disaster, and I had gradually gotten used to him. In some ways he was like an extra-large child, evoking sympathy and goodwill once you got past his formidable appearance. Even so, the reaction of the general public meeting him for the first time was understandable. In the settled order of things, seven feet, no eyebrows, and no clothes can be rather shocking.

After several months of subsisting in this environment, I started to feel restless and ill at ease. One afternoon I walked up the side of a volcano, and sat myself down for a bit of a think. Gazing out towards the beckoning South Seas, I slowly digested the idea that the realities of permanent travel were out of my league. It was time to get another life. During the course of that afternoon, I gradually eased into the gentler realm of tourism, and started making plans to return to the mainland.

Peter the Giant wasn't coming back.

But to return to Annapurna. In the evening I got out of my little cocoon and went downstairs, hoping to warm up by the kitchen fire for a while. However, the drizzling dampness of the day had by now worked its way into the firewood supply as well, and the kitchen 'fire' was pretty much stuck in the conceptual stage. It was going to be iodine and water for dinner for me. The prospect of eating semi-cooked food in this place was setting off alarm bells.

I was probably being a mite over-squeamish, not to say paranoid, about the food. On the other hand, after many years of experience with giardia and a broad sampling of assorted other stomach crud, maybe I wasn't. Most of the food on the menus in these lodges is usually fine, but the food preparation operation can be another matter. For example, the cutting boards in some of these places are rarely, if ever, washed, and the dish towel on hand to dry off your plate often looks like it was used to wipe down the yak out in the yard before being pressed into service in the kitchen.

And it might well have been. A few years before in the Upper Mustang region, my traveling companion was being careful about her eating as well. One evening we arrived at a spanking new lodge, so new it wasn't actually finished yet. Everything in the place looked fresh and clean and just unpacked, until we got to the no-frills mountain kitchen. After seeing what that looked like, my friend decided she would order a dish of plain rice. According to standard practice at these altitudes, this was going to be made in a pressure cooker. And surely, food doesn't get much cleaner or more sterilized than that, one would think. Not exactly. The spoon that was provided to serve the rice from the pressure cooker on to the plate had been conveniently placed in the yak dung that was used for fuel sitting in a box next to the stove.

Within a few hours, she was well and truly ill, vomiting violently and repeatedly. There were no toilets connected inside the lodge as of yet, and the front door had been locked for the night. Fortunately, our room was on the ground floor, and she was the right size to squeeze through the narrow window. She spent most of that night climbing in and out, and throwing up in the backyard. Which goes to show that even if one does try to be careful about what one eats, there is no sure-fire guarantee that you won't get sick anyway.

Nevertheless, despite such a rough night, she

woke up early the following morning according to the originally established plan, and put in a full day's march without a word of complaint, several substantial and wind-bound passes withal. Hats off to a really sturdy traveler.

12

Clothes make the man.
Naked people have little or no influence in society.

Mark Twain (attributed)

As I proceeded upwards along the AC (Annapurna Circuit), I was giving away packets of seeds that had remained unplanted in my most recent garden; things like zinnias, sunflowers, morning glories, spinach, and an assortment of herbs. Judging by the flourishing state of her flowers and vegetables, I decided that this innkeeper knew a thing or two about plants. While I was drinking the morning's coffee and settling the bill, I handed her the last packet I had left, some basil seeds from France. At first, she was unsure exactly what they were, as basil is not commonly grown in this area. When I explained that it was an essential ingredient for the pasta she made for the guests, she was very appreciative, and I walked on confident that they had found a good home.

This was one of my favorite types of walking days. The fogs and showers of the day before had now moved on, the weather was cool and dry, and the sky was overcast and gray. I started out slowly, heading for Chame, yesterday's original destination. *Chame* means something close to 'sunny fields by the cliffs'. This village is the district center, one of its main markets, and the most sophisticated place on this part of the trail, with a boarding school, a police station, a clinic, and a jail. Chame also has several banks that will exchange foreign currency, and a number of well-provisioned pharmacies and general stores. I returned to the same lodge that I had once stayed in on my first trip up here many years ago before the coming of the road. The lodge itself was basically unchanged, but the village was somewhat larger and much cleaner, now that all the horse trains had gone.

My supply of rupees was running low, so an open exchange bank was a welcome find. I changed some money, and then I strolled around seeing the sights and doing some shopping. Among other things, I was looking for some much-wanted mouthwash, but there didn't seem to be any available in the central shops. Eventually I hit upon the bright idea of trying to make my own by combining some disinfectant with soda water. Yuck. What a revolting, toxic concoction that was. This distinctly less than spearmint result was quickly spat out, but it had thoroughly scalded the inside of my mouth. Those disinfectant makers know what they are talking about when they say *for external use only*. Henceforth I would be sticking to the store-bought variety.

This section coming up to Chame was more thought-provoking than I had expected. The trails of Nepal are home to large numbers of professional porters who bring the necessities of life to distant villages. The massive loads that these diminutive mountain people regularly carry are truly remarkable: huge piles of firewood, multiple sacks of cement, two-meter sections of fifty-centimeter steel pipe, industrial refrigerators, fifty-kilo bags of flour, pairs of full gas cylinders, ten or more sheets of four-by-eight-foot plywood, bulky rolls of galvanized tin roofing, nested stacks of metal beds, or about eight cases of Foster's, would be some common examples.

To help them better manage these heavy burdens,

there are raised platforms called *chautaras* built of neat stonework at frequent distances all along the trail. Most of these resting stations are circular, sometimes they are rectangular, and there is often a banyan planted in the middle to provide some welcoming shade. These structures feature a wide shelf set at the same height that the loads are carried. When porters need to take a break or stop for meals, they back up to one of these shelves and gently set down their loads behind them. This is a far more convenient and effective way for them to get in and out of their harnesses than continually shifting such massive loads up and down off the ground would be.

I once tried to lift one of these loads that was sitting on a *chautara* at the entrance of our lunch stop village. Its owner had left it there on the shelf and gone for tea nearby. This load consisted of three or four steel suspension bridge sections, each one about a meter long. I could hardly move the thing. I can't imagine what carrying it all day must have been like. These loads might stagger your imagination, but not these tough Nepalese porters. In addition, since I am quite a bit taller than most of the local people, these shelves make comfortable trailside seats with excellent backrests.

About halfway to Chame, there was a humorous

incident. I was idling at one of these platforms catching my breath on one of the longer steep sections (this was still early days here). While I was resting there on the shelf, a party of well-heeled European tourists hove into view, advancing laboriously up the path. These people had clearly not spared any expense in equipping themselves. They had the best boots money can buy, brand-new, top-of-the-range backpacks with airflow-enabling, carbon frames, advanced design, shock-absorbing trekking poles, GPS guidance apps, and state-of-the-art, friction-cutting outerwear: the whole, high-tech nine yards. As they struggled slowly on up the hill, along came a petite local granny wearing a homemade sweater, a cotton sarong, and cheap plastic flip-flops, and smoked by them with twenty-five kilos of rice strapped to her back. My take-away from all this was somewhere between mildly amused and decidedly impressed.

Revealing *East meets West* moments like this are unpredictable but not uncommon when you are traveling in these regions. You step into them now and again in unexpected places. One of the earliest and most striking examples that I can remember happened in North Africa when I was in about the eighth or ninth grade. As it turns out, this one also involved clothing and apparel.

At that time, my father was working in a remote oil camp on the coast of Libya, refining various petroleum products and loading crude and LNG onto tankers anchored offshore. Putting it mildly, this camp was very basic. There was almost nothing there. (For a more thorough and detailed description, you can consult my long-suffering mother, who endured all this stark desolation through many long years for our sake.) Realizing that the sanity of their employees was likely to fray in such a minimal environment, the oil company running the camp set out to provide things for them to do during leisure hours. They built tennis courts and swimming pools and bowling alleys; they organized billiards clubs and lending libraries; they opened some restaurants and cinemas and hairdressing salons. And, with one of their more ambitious visions, they created a golf course.

To do this, a suitably extensive acreage next to the shoreline was selected and surveyed. Bulldozers and road graders were put to work flattening and smoothing long stretches of dunes to make the fairways. These were then covered with truckloads of brown, ribbon-like seaweed collected from the beaches, which were plowed into the sand to make a spongey, semi-vegetable layer about six inches thick. And at the ends of these avenues, they put the 'greens', with appropriate metal holes and flags set in the middle. These 'greens' were not actually green, however. They made these by combining sand with crude oil to form a substance that was about the same color and texture as cinnamon toast mixture – 'browns', as it were. Because it was wide and spacious, usually empty, and not far from our houses, this makeshift golf course soon became one of the favorite haunts of us expatriate kids. Whenever we had nothing much else to do, we would often drift out there and hang around.

Every once in a while, several families from the camp would pile into their cars and make the four-hour drive over to Benghazi for some much-needed variety and entertainment. At that time, Benghazi was a colorful fusion of a modern Italian sea port and an old North African market town, with prolific souks that were nearly endless. Excursions like these were always fun and interesting. On one of these trips to the souks, I had acquired a complete set of traditional Bedouin clothing and carted it back to the camp. Not long afterwards, I put it on and headed out for a ramble over the golf course to try it out. I was wearing a loose, ankle-length cotton robe, the classic Arab headdress with gilded, be-tasseled cords to hold it in place, shades, and bare feet: a Lawrence of Arabia fantasy in full tilt.

A while later, somewhere out on the golf course, I encountered a middle-aged Libyan gentleman carrying a very expensive-looking set of shiny new golf clubs, and sporting a fairly comprehensive golf costume: two-tone golf shoes with turf spikes, performance stretch pants, stylish polo shirt, mesh baseball cap, leather golf gloves, etc., clearly zeroing in on the pro look. He could well have just stepped off the film set for a golf movie.

I was a young moron out on a mindless romp. This dude, however, appeared to be engaged in something rather more purposeful. For him, strutting about in full-on golf array was important business. It looked like the game itself didn't really matter all that much to him – the role-playing was the main thing here. This was a thoroughgoing exercise in international identity development. When I greeted him in Arabic as I passed by, he eyed me askance with a displeased, caught-in-the-act sort of look. It was as if we had been set down in front of full-length mirrors out there in the dunes. I think we both understood at about the same instant just how silly we looked.

I was just a dumb kid fooling around with a potential Halloween costume, so this wasn't really a big deal. He, however, was a lot closer to that age when, as Dostoyevsky once put it, it is difficult not to take yourself rather seriously. As I wandered on across the springy carpet of seaweed and sand, I sensed that this brief meeting had made him more than a little uncomfortable. In the famous words of Rudyard Kipling:

> Oh, East is East, and West is West,
> and never the twain shall meet;

even when both sides are energetically faking it.

13

The sleep of the laboring man is sweet,
whether he eat little or much.

Ecclesiastes 5:12

Today I began the long, two-day segment from Chame under the cliffs up to Manang. Manang is the main center in this higher country around Thorung La Pass, and the one from which this region takes its name. This town is also a bit unusual compared to most of the others in the Nepali hinterlands in that its citizens have long been international traders and dealmakers. Many of these Manangis travel widely abroad and maintain business connections all over Asia and beyond. They have a reputation for shrewdness and hard bargaining.

In this section you walk past the panoramic *Panungda Danda*, the grand wall of Pisang, a massive, sweeping cliff face that rises almost vertically for more than a kilometer from the riverbed on the right side of the valley. This striking landmark is a popular sight for pilgrimages and religious observances with the local people. This was my first real walking day, a distance of around sixteen kilometers or so, much of it steadily uphill within earshot of the river. Sixteen kilometers is not a very long day by local standards, but in my seriously overweight and out of shape condition, coming directly from a life of advanced couch sluggery, it was taxing.

About lunchtime, a Spanish couple sitting in a trailside tea house recommended that I head for the village of Upper Pisang, instead of the lower one as I was planning to do. This was an auspicious development. The amended and much prettier route followed a small path winding on through fields of flowering buckwheat, tennis-court-sized explosions of bright pink flowers inside neat, waist-high stone walls. Upper Pisang is across the valley from the lower village. This location has a much better view of the towering pinnacles on the other side. About dinner time, the clouds opened for a short interval, and we saw Annapurna II bathed in the sunset far above.

What a presence. These mountains are so high, and constructed on such a dramatic scale, they look almost unreal and dreamlike, as if they were special effects made for an epic fantasy film. The altitude of Upper Pisang is a little over three thousand meters, but the windswept crown of Annapurna II is around eight thousand meters, soaring almost five kilometers straight up before the village. The upper parts of this great peak were completely white, deeply blanketed in the unblemished monsoon snows. I sat there with the Spanish people in the dining room looking upward at the reddening summit, feeling very small.

On the second day I continued onwards from Upper Pisang towards Manang town itself. In this area, the pine forest thins out, the high desert tundra zone begins, and many things become distinctively Tibetan. The landscape, the houses, the clothing, the diet, the religion, and the cultural heritage are very similar to those just over the border, which is only a short distance away. Mani walls, prayer wheels, arched chortens, black gowns, homemade woolen boots, and seasoned, leathery complexions start to appear frequently from here onwards.

This was another long day for me, almost twenty kilometers. By noon I was getting hungry, but I was still apprehensive about eating most of the things on the tea house menus, except for the uninteresting and not very appetizing standbys like boiled eggs, fried macaroni, and plain rice I had been mostly sticking to thus far. You can go a long way on these safe staples, but by then I was starting to get somewhat tired of them. Another installment of this same bill of fare did not appeal to me at all just then.

However, at a guest house in the village of Hongde about midday, I discovered an as yet untried delicacy that I was reasonably confident would not lay me out on my bed. There in the unwashed and dusty tea house window sat a large can of 'made in India' baked beans, stamped with an expiration date that had not yet passed, no less. The innkeeper heated them up on her wood stove, and I fell to. An American traveler sitting nearby watching this quiet celebration wryly observed: *Well, at least you'll get your sodium.*

Believe me, at this point a balanced diet and healthy food choices were not exactly front and center on my list of priorities. I was starving, and that was absolutely, definitely the most wonderfully appetizing dish of sodium I have ever bolted down.

I arrived in Manang at about three o'clock, and checked into the Tilicho Hotel, last seen years ago with a four-foot mantle of snow and ice covering the roof. This time I took advantage of the warmer season and took a hot shower, something I had hesitated to do at three and a half thousand meters in late January. I had not seen a mirror in many days. Stepping in front of one to brush my teeth was a bit of a surprise. It is stunning what you can turn into, and how quickly, when grooming is neglected, even briefly.

All spruced up, I went out and wandered around the town until happy hour. Nearby I found a man with a new washing machine and a price list for doing various items of clothing, which was a surprise of a more welcome sort. Nothing like this had been available some years before, and I was delighted to give him most of my pack. Let's face it, washing stuff by hand in the sink may tide you over for a while, but laundry that has been worn on the trail doesn't really get clean like that. It just looks a little less awful.

Also notable is how well you sleep when you walk long distances. In my former working life, it was altogether too common to retire at a normal time, and then just lie there wide awake, tossing and turning, unable to sleep for hours, either from stress, or lack of exercise, or too much caffeine, information overload, or whatever. When I have walked all day, on the other hand, I am pretty much out for the count as soon as my head hits the pillow.

14

Take your rest, Teacher.

Advice from students

On these rugged, steep paths, as on most long-distance trails, it is not wise to just keep on pounding out miles day after day. You need to take breaks periodically, to restore your energy levels, rest your feet, and regroup mentally. And, this being the Himalayas, you also have to be ever mindful of the altitude. If you fall into the surprisingly common *have to keep going no matter what* mentality, you can get way too high, much too fast. I needed to pause in Manang for a while and acclimatize before going any higher. A day of rest was in order.

Accordingly, on this day I did very little. I had a latish, leisurely breakfast, and then lounged about in my room, cleaned my boots, and started reading a new book I found in the breakfast hall, *Jane Eyre*.

There was no possibility of taking a walk that day,

as Ms. Brontë said. Eventually I drifted off to sleep around lunchtime. When I awoke later in the afternoon, I went out to explore the village and see what changes the last decade had wrought.

As I had never been here during the summer before, some of the first things to draw my attention were the thriving vegetable gardens. Almost every house here was surrounded by nicely tended patches of spinach, cabbages, bok choy, onions, and pumpkins, flanked by dense clusters of chives and cilantro. Seeing all this vibrant, mouth-watering produce, I realized how far short of the higher cuisine I was falling with my austere, paranoia-prompted regime of eggs and plain rice (and now perhaps baked beans, if I could find some more of those cans). I missed my kitchen and my wok.

The flower gardens were eye-catching as well. In spite of the high altitude, there were plenty of cosmos and hollyhocks in assorted shades of pink and white, and long beds of deep red and yellow marigolds on all sides. One lodge even had an impressive stand of sturdy, two-and-a-half-foot-tall opium poppies blooming prolifically next to the front gate. The plump, green balls on the tops of the stems looked like they were about ready for the three-pronged knife.

They plant themselves, the innkeeper said. Also planting themselves were lots and lots of large and vigorous-looking marijuana bushes, along the edges of the narrow lanes, inside the vegetable plots and the empty lots, around the borders of the fields, and in the hotel yards. It was everywhere.

I was pleased to see that the new road had not had that much of an effect. It was not much more than a wide trail here. The entrance to the village that passed through an arched chorten, and the stone lanes between the buildings following after it, were just too narrow for jeeps. What few vehicles there were had been left outside of the town in a field at the bottom of the hill.

However, a very noticeable difference since my last visit was the advent of mobile technology. Almost everyone in sight now had a mobile phone. Shopkeepers, hotel workers, tottering grannies, goat herders, trail guides, the humblest, poorest porters in near rags and bare feet, young schoolchildren, and even pre-school children were all staring at their mobile phones. Most of the teenage employees who were working at the hotel were especially absorbed in this pursuit. Pausing to assist hotel guests was clearly a resented intrusion. This was unexpected. The Nepalese have a well-deserved reputation for being some of the kindest, friendliest, and most helpful people you will meet anywhere. This surly *don't bother me I am on my phone* stance was new, and distinctly out of character.

Not very long ago, it was the normal practice of trekkers, guides, and hotel owners to gather around the wood stove in the common room of an evening, sipping tea and beer and hot rakshi, the potent, home-brewed local moonshine. The dinner hours were usually spent chatting, meeting new people, exchanging insights about the conditions and the lodges ahead, forecasting the coming weather, and so forth. This made for a convivial and relaxing atmosphere after the day's exertions along the trail. This doesn't happen that much anymore, however. Nowadays, almost everyone in the dining room is glued to their phone, locked into their own private space. Hardly anyone talks. Most of the people just sit there looking at pictures of themselves, watching films, or surfing by the hour, without saying a word to the people around them.

I realize that this is a generational phenomenon, but I do find this quite strange. For many of these folks, the stuff on their phones seems to be more real to them than their actual physical surroundings. A selfie with snow-clad Annapurna in the background has more substance and interest for them than the actual mountain itself in view right outside the door. I don't think this is very healthy. Curmudgeon that I am, I do sometimes ask loud phone addicts to please turn their devices down, if they wouldn't mind. And usually they will do so quite politely. However, it is nearly impossible to make such a request when an entire roomful is thus engaged. As a result, all too often these days, many of the common rooms in the lodges are no longer pleasant places to unwind. Although there are still some wonderfully congenial and hospitable exceptions to that, sadly, this is now the prevailing trend.

When the Wi-Fi connection crashes, as it not infrequently does up in the hills, then you get a lodge full of semi-disoriented people who are not quite sure what to do next. Delegations of worried guests appear at the front desk to have a conversation something like this one, in a blend of frustration and concerned incredulity:

> Hotel Guest: Um, excuse me, ah, the Wi-Fi isn't working now?
> Hotel Manager: No, it's not. I'm sorry.
> Hotel Guest: Do you know when it's going to come back on?
> Hotel Manager: No, I'm afraid we don't. Maybe later in the day.
> Hotel Guest: Oh, my!

Unfortunately, it looks like this mentality is now quickly becoming the 'new normal', and not just in the distance-walking milieu. It's very widespread. In my recent life over in the Gulf, I had a fishing boat, and I regularly took colleagues and friends out to sea for a day of deep-sea fishing, picnicking on sand bars, dolphin-watching, and such like. When you come in from a day like that, dockside etiquette has long been that guests stick around for half an hour or so, and help the owner clean up the boat and put it away. Trailering a fishing boat smoothly is normally more than a one-person job, and most of these guests stayed and helped, or at least offered to.

But not the phone freaks. They were desperate to go home as soon as they could and post their dolphin selfies right away. They couldn't do this from the boat on the way back because network coverage extended only a few kilometers offshore. For them, helping me get the boat out of the water was out of the question. In their minds, the trip was not real until it was recorded online. It had little value beyond what it could do to enhance their media profiles.

Sorry, Captain, got to go… I have to get back to my screen!

This does not bode well.

15

For want of a nail the shoe was lost;
For want of a shoe the horse was lost;
For want of a horse the rider was lost.

George Herbert

Leaving Manang there was a choice of several routes to follow. One path ascended a side valley to the west up towards Lake Tilicho, a secluded alpine lake about a two-day walk away. At five thousand meters, this is one of the highest lakes in the world, set in a desolate arena of immense slopes of scree and cragged icy peaks. The other option was the actual Annapurna Circuit itself, which takes you from Manang into the really high country around Thorung La Pass. I decided to go to Lake Tilicho first, because the altitude there is somewhat lower than it is nearer to Thorung La. This would give my system a few extra days to adapt to the elevation, which can be so critical up here.

There was an unexpected and sobering episode involving my hat. During monsoon time up in the hills, a lot of days are clear and sunny early in the morning. About mid-morning, thick clouds begin to gather, and then somewhere between one and two p.m., the daily rains begin. Adjusted for this pattern, the usual plan is to start walking early and get to the day's destination before the downpour arrives.

When I left the lodge about seven thirty, the sunlight was strong and bright, so I put on my sun hat as I was making my way out of the village. The trail here was very wet and rocky, and I was looking down at the ground as I went, trying hard to avoid stepping in puddles and stumbling on the uneven footing. Because of the downward angle of my gaze, I walked right past a prominent signpost directing me to make a hard-right turn at the end of the village without seeing it at all. The wide brim of my hat blocked out the sign completely, and I continued going straight ahead on another trail. Eventually a kind yak herdsman walking along with his drove turned me around, but by this time I had walked several hours in the wrong direction, and I was now seriously behind the daily rain schedule. As a result, contrary to usual practice, I was still on the trail in the afternoon when the rains began, and I was caught in a most stupendous and drenching monsoon thunderstorm, quite possibly the heaviest one of the whole trip.

Happily, my passport was wrapped in a sandwich bag at the time, so it stayed dry, but its owner was not so fortunate. In the midst of this deluge, I came to a place where the trail was only a narrow, downward-slanting shelf of rock protruding from a cliff, now slick with the rain. I was not liking the look of this at all, but I couldn't see another way past this treacherous section. Slowly and carefully, I began inching along the shelf. About two thirds of the way across, I lost my footing and took a hard fall onto my back. Fortunately, I fell backwards against the cliff, and not over the edge, as I very easily could have done.

Now here's the thing. If I had delayed putting on my hat for a few minutes that morning, I would have seen that sign on the way out of town, and would not have arrived in this dangerous place in the driving rain. I would have passed this section earlier when the shelf was still dry, and would most probably have been sitting in a lodge sipping a hot toddy by this time, instead of stretched on my back on the rocks, soaked to the skin, very lucky not to be lying somewhere below with a broken leg. What a huge difference such small things can make.

Here is another example of the life-altering power of minor events, which, incidentally, also features the perils of head gear. For a number of years, my brother was working in mid-town Manhattan, and living in an apartment not far from Greenwich Village. To keep fit, he liked to rise early and go for a bracing bicycle ride before starting his day. One morning in October, he got up, carried his bicycle down to the sidewalk, and set off. However, when he got to the corner of his street, he realized that he had forgotten to take his helmet. He paused, pondered this for a moment, and then decided it would be best to go get it. He went back to his apartment, picked up the helmet, and set out once again.

A little while later, as he was cruising along down Fifth Avenue, the driver of a city bus had a seizure and collapsed at the wheel. The now driverless bus went careening down the street at forty miles an hour, and slammed my brother against a building, leaving him only minutes away from being dead. Fortunately, this had happened very early on a national holiday, and the streets were empty. An emergency crew from a mid-town hospital managed to reach him in time, and he is still with us today, bringing joy and nicely written news to us all. If he had not been wearing that helmet, he would most probably have been killed immediately. However, consider this: If he had not gone back to his apartment to get the helmet, he would not have been at that spot when the bus crashed into him. Which compellingly and rather eerily puts one in mind of Somerset Maugham's one-page short story called 'The Appointment in Samarra'. You do need to be careful with these hats.

Eventually I arrived in Khangsar, a small community about halfway to the base camp for Lake Tilicho. This little village soon distinguished itself in several interesting ways. One of them was how much simpler and unadorned it was, compared to the villages lower down. It was just a small collection of flat-roofed, Tibetan-style stone houses clustered together one right next to another on the steep side of the mountain. The roofs were heaped with long stacks of roughly chopped firewood (winter is never far away at this height); there was hardly anything that looked modern in sight, and no cars. Most of the houses appeared to have crude-looking, DIY electric wiring and jerry-rigged plumbing, and they had been left in the natural stone shades of gray and brown.

Almost nothing was painted. The village looked like it was part of the rocky hillside, the way Tibetan villages appear in old black-and-white photographs of this region. In many ways, the ancient, high-altitude, subsistence-farming life of Tibet was still happening here.

Another notable feature of the place quickly became apparent as well. Unlike the people in Manang, no one here was carrying a mobile phone. My guess was that there was probably no coverage. However, instead of the usual mobile phones, most of the people I encountered were carrying some type of flask: plastic water bottles, assortments of soft drink containers, beer bottles of various sizes and brands, old jars, and such like. I wondered about this for a while, and then I twigged: These folks were gearing up for an imminent, village-wide happy hour. Mothers with small babies, young people hanging about in the streets, shopkeepers sitting on their doorsteps, porters done with their loads, oldsters huddling next to wood stoves, and my hotel manager: Nearly everybody in sight had a generous measure of rakshi close to hand. I checked into my modest room, took off my wet clothes, and lay down to take a nap after the excitements and surprises of a hard day. When I awoke an hour or so later, almost the whole place was drinking.

It is remarkable how popular alcohol has been down through the ages. Even in the most primitive societies, where people have almost nothing, there is usually something fermented available to drink. I have often wondered how this beloved drug was first discovered. Perhaps it could have happened something along these lines. Some of our distant ancestors deep in the mists of antiquity went out hunting and gathering one day and came upon a patch of ripe wild grapes. They carried several loads of them back to their settlement, and put them in earthenware or wooden vessels of some sort. This stockpile took a while to eat, during which time some of the grapes sitting near the bottom of the jars were crushed by the weight of the ones above them, and the yeast that lives naturally on the skins of the grapes went to work on the resulting slush. Eventually, when all of the grapes had been finished, someone who was overseeing the jars noticed some leftover juice at the bottom and tried a mouthful or two. Eyes blazed, the neighbors were called out, and happy hour and the wine industry were born. And lordy-lord have they thrived ever since, not least in remote hamlets like Khangsar.

If this place was deprived in some ways, it was handsomely endowed in others. Khangsar was rich in mice. The ceilings and the lower half of the walls in my room were made of thin plywood. The upper part was just a few colored sheets tacked to studs to cover the stones. The whole time I was in there, from the late afternoon when I moved in until early the next morning when I left, gangs of mice chased each other around inside the walls, and scurried relentlessly across the ceiling panels. The sheets were continually popping and bulging as the mice behind crashed into them. I did not sleep very well in that room. The noise of the mice kept me awake most of the night. As I lay there in the darkness longing for daylight, I considered the weighty question of which was preferable: to have a whole village addicted to the internet to an extent endangering basic civility, or a whole village addicted to the local rotgut to an extent endangering basic well-being. Tough call.

16

Life is fraught with peril and inconvenience.

Folk saying

When the sun finally came up, my one desire in life was to get out of that room as fast as I could. I stuffed everything into my pack, paid the bill, and got right back on the trail without stopping to have breakfast, or even my usual morning coffee. The mice were seriously creeping me out.

This was a mistake. A standard feature of most of the trails in Nepal is their tendency to keep going up and up, and then still up some more, steeply and relentlessly, sometimes all day. You plod on from one bend to the next, climbing one slope after another. Then, hope springing eternal, you are sure that around the next turn, things will finally start to level off. But when you actually get there, yet another arduous climb appears in front of you. To sustain this constant ascent with any sort of grace, you really do need some carbs and a good, solid dose of caffeine. Walking these paths without sleep and without breakfast is not a good plan.

Eventually the soaring beauty around me began to disperse the low-energy funk brought on by the rushed departure. High above on the other side of the valley were the immense snow fields of Annapurna I itself, awash in early morning sun, with long, graceful waterfalls that resembled fine-spun silver threads hanging down from the lofty cliffs, the Khangsar Khola rushing far below, and seas of pretty wild flowers bobbing gently in the wind. Breakfast or no breakfast, this part of the world was meant to be.

However, in addition to being beautiful and exhilarating, the path became increasingly unstable and exposed as I proceeded. After a few kilometers it turned into an eight-inch-wide ribbon cutting across long, sheer expanses of loose scree studded with van-sized boulders that did not look all that solid. A misstep here could easily launch you into a crashing plunge over the side. If you were to fall off the trail here, you would immediately slide away towards the distant river, and it might be a while before anyone found you down there, especially if your super-loud emergency whistle has been conveniently forgotten at home, like mine had been. It would take a formidable effort to climb back up such a prodigious slope of almost vertical scree, even if you were uninjured. This concept tends to focus the mind, and the eyesight, very much on your footing. There were lots and lots of very careful baby steps in this section.

Gravity and loose stones withal, eventually I arrived at Tilicho Base Camp without incident, and headed on towards the lake early the next morning. However, even though I took some Diamox at breakfast, about three quarters of the way up I started to experience the warning symptoms of altitude trouble: headache, nausea, difficulty breathing, wobbly balance, lassitude. Disappointed, but realizing that I was not sufficiently acclimatized to go to five thousand meters safely, I decided it would probably be better to descend, and try this again in a day or two. One should not trifle with AMS (acute mountain sickness) in the Himalayas.

Sometimes I am asked if I worry about the dangers of walking alone in remote places like this.

Am I not concerned about risks to my personal safety, either because of injury, or as a result of foul play? The answer to such questions is: Yes, I am. Falls are always possible, and I have taken some rather nasty ones over the years. However, the danger from falls can be considerably reduced by going slowly, watching where you step, and walking only in daylight. I am careful. And as far as foul play is concerned, untoward surprises do happen now and then. You do encounter some dangerous people some of the time. However, most of the really unsavory incidents that have come my way have happened in much more heavily populated areas.

Case in point, some years back I was staying in Peshawar up in northern Pakistan, close to the Afghan border. In those days, a while before the Afghans started fleeing in their millions from the harsh Russian invasion, Peshawar was a small, conservative district hub on the edge of the northern tribal areas. Tribal folks and hill men came here to buy fruits and vegetables in its extensive markets, and hardware from the historic manufacturing bazaar.

This remarkable bazaar was in the same league as the ancient working souk of Aleppo, which has now sadly been destroyed. Anything these tough villagers could ever want or require was being made here: their heavy-duty, hill country sandals; flat, Afghan-style woolen hats; custom tailored clothing; blankets; garden tools; pruning hooks; saddles; harnesses; bullet belts; holsters; wolf traps; earthenware; cauldrons; knives; axes; horse shoes; baskets; tents; bird cages; some of the best shish kebab in the whole world, and all manner of guns, to give a small sampling. This humming souk produced simply everything, and was by far the busiest, the most fascinating, and the most medieval bazaar I have ever seen. The whole place breathed the spirit of the old Silk Road like nowhere else I know of, especially in the winter, dusted in falling snow. It even had a functioning caravanserai still looking much as it had centuries ago.

At this time, foreigners and tourists were not all that common in Peshawar. Many of the local townspeople, and especially the residents of the outlying villages, were not used to seeing Westerners, and when they encountered one, they were quite curious. As a result, whenever Western travelers stopped on the street to examine merchandise or to purchase something, a crowd of inquisitive local people and hill types immediately gathered around them. These folks didn't want anything; they didn't say anything. They just stood there about a foot away, and silently gawked until the foreigner moved on. Westerners have pretty firm expectations about their personal, physical space. Our comfort zone requires that there be a certain amount of room between us and others. To suddenly find yourself with none is disconcerting. This is especially unnerving when a mass of people enclosing you consists of rough-hewn, full-bearded Pathan tribesmen sporting gold teeth, loaded bandoliers, and long knives.

At first, these incessant crowds made me rather uneasy, but in time I gradually got used to them. There was one event in particular that made these knots of local people seem like just a normal part of being in the bazaar. One morning I came across a keen-eyed, itinerant tradesman be-draped with small, silver hearts on black, necklace-length ribbons. He had hundreds of these trinkets hanging from his arms and his neck, and as he slowly progressed through the narrow lanes, he was chanting their price, in the time-honored fashion of street hawkers in the East. After following me around for a bit, he decided that the dense crowds collecting near me were a prime commercial opportunity.

One rupee contains a hundred pice, or cents. Twenty-five pice is four annas, eight annas is fifty pice, or half a rupee, and so forth. The price for one of these little hearts was four annas, which was a small, silver coin in those days. In Urdu, four annas is *char anna*. As this fellow walked along, he was resonantly chanting: *Char anna, char anna, char anna, char char annaaaay!* with the last syllable emphasized and extended. He fell into step with me, and wherever I happened to stop, he plied the instantly forming mobs with the ribbons. Boosted by the unusual, curiosity-awakening presence of an outlandish tourist, sales were moving at the proverbial hot cake level.

I found all this rather amusing, and after a few blocks, I decided to take a more active part in these proceedings. I hung several handfuls of these necklaces from my arms as well, and joined in the price song with him. Now the two of us were ambling along, chanting *char anna* together, and the numbers of onlookers increased apace, as the childlike people poured out of their buildings to see what was doing. This playful procession continued for several hours until his stock of hearts ran out, and our pockets were heavy with silver. This had been an exceptionally delightful and memorable morning for both of us. After that day, these constant, encircling gangs were not that intimidating any more, and I just went about my business without paying much attention to them or monitoring their moods. This turned out to be a very serious lapse of judgement.

One afternoon some weeks later, I stopped by a fruit vendor, and another one of these packs formed in the usual manner. But this time, without any warning, this bunch suddenly boiled over and exploded into violence. They threw me on the ground and started kicking the crap out of me with their rugged, tribal footwear. I was really getting stomped out there. This continued for some minutes until the police arrived and broke up the crowd with their bamboo lathis. Some concerned citizen must have rung them up right away (many blessings upon you).

The police were most gracious and gentlemanly. They put me in a rickshaw and took me down to the nearby Peshawar city jail. They very politely explained that I was not under arrest, but that it would be best if I spent the night there under their protection. The town was charged with a strange, volatile mood that day, and they were concerned that the crowd they had dispersed might try this again if I went back to my hotel.

As it turned out, their premonitions were not mistaken. A short time after this, my traveling companions were assaulted by another crew a few blocks away. The police had to go rescue them as well, and brought them to the jail for safe keeping a little while later. They served us dinner, and then escorted us to some cells to sleep in. The following morning, the officers decided that it would be wise for us to leave town as soon as possible. They escorted us back to our hotel to round up our luggage, and then drove us to the station. We got out of Dodge on the next train. Looking back on this event, we were very lucky with how all this turned out. This happened several generations ago. The world was not as angry and extremist back then as it is now. In the same situation today, we could well have been killed.

Another time, I was passing through Istanbul on the way back to Europe. One evening I went out to dinner in the center of town near the Taksim Square area. When I came out of the restaurant, it was getting rather late, and I thought it might be unwise to walk home through the dimly lit streets to my building a few kilometers away. I hailed what I took to be a *dolmush*, a big shared taxi cruising back and forth between fixed points of the city. This was a black, antique Packard like the one my father used to drive in the forties, containing three or four other passengers. However, this was no *dolmush*, and the other people in it were not passengers. This was a carload of thugs cruising the tourist section hoping to hijack tipsy foreigners making their way home late at night, just as I was then doing.

Liquored up as I was, it took a minute or two for me to understand what was actually happening. Then I braced myself to bail out as soon as the car slowed down for a turn. Anticipating my intention, one of the lads up in the front jumped on top of me and pinned me firmly to the back seat. They took me out to a remote field somewhere on the edge of the city and proceeded to rob me. They took my belt (not a money belt); they took my watch (a cheap piece of junk from a street stall); they took my faded jacket (Goodwill's finest); and they took my wallet (empty).

These fellows were pissed. Instead of a wealthy businessman or a well-heeled tourist like they were expecting, these clowns had grabbed a penniless hippie. They spent more money on the gas for this abortive little enterprise than anything they took from me was remotely worth. However, I was lucky this time as well. Instead of getting violent, they just dumped me in the mud and drove away. Eventually some passing Turkish soldiers discovered me wandering around out there in the dark and drove me back into town (peace be upon them). Again, that was a different time. In these more radicalized days we live in now, things might not have turned out as harmlessly as they did.

To conclude, scary, unpleasant things such as these do sometimes happen when you travel around by yourself. There are definitely some very nasty people out there. However, most of the truly dangerous stuff usually tends to happen in urban areas, and not on remote trails in the hills.

17

They that be whole need not a physician,
but they that are sick.

Matthew 9:12

Another subject that sometimes generates enquiries is physical health. Occasionally I am asked things like: *Are you concerned about your health on these walks? Aren't you worried about medical emergencies? What would happen if you got sick out there?*

This is also something I think about periodically. However, serious concerns such as these are tempered by several mitigating factors. One of them is that I eat and drink very cautiously, some might say a bit too cautiously, when I travel, as we have already seen. This usually makes a big difference in how often you get sick in these places. I also carry an ample first aid kit. I always take antibiotics, diarrhea pills, eye drops, painkillers, cold medicines, antiseptics, ear balm, bandages, anti-acids, cough lozenges, clove oil, and the like. This stuff sack takes up a gallon of pack space and probably weighs about two kilos. I am usually pretty well prepared for much of the stuff that is likely to happen out there on the trail.

Another consideration is that in most of the world, the medical situation is not nearly as draconian as it is in America. Most countries don't take the same approach to medical matters that America follows. For example, let's suppose a workman in the United States who cannot afford medical insurance loses some fingers in an accident. If he goes to the hospital to have them re-attached, he may well end up struggling to pay the resulting bill for most of his life. And this way of doing things is commonly viewed as standard operating procedure, no pun intended. However, in almost all of the rest of the world, civilized governments normally consider it to be their clear responsibility and bounden duty to provide reasonably priced or free medical care for all of their citizens. Benevolent and enlightened policies like this are very helpful for us travelers as well.

Some years ago, I crossed the border from Afghanistan into Iran, on my way from Herat down to Tehran. A few days after I had arrived in Tehran, I woke up with bright yellow eyes and urine that looked like black coffee. Something serious was plainly amiss. The main branch of the university hospital was nearby, so I went over there and presented myself at the ER desk. They took a quick look at me and said: *You have hepatitis. Get in bed.*

The hospital put me into a private room in the infectious disease ward so I would not pass this stuff on to anyone else. For four or five weeks they provided me with medicine and care, around-the-clock personal attention, hot showers, laundry service, color TV, and three good meals a day. They were invariably kind and polite, and highly professional in everything they did. I felt more like an honored guest than a patient.

By and by the nurse came to the room one morning, and told me that the critical phase of the disease had passed, and that I could now go home and finish recuperating there. I packed a shopping bag with a few personal odds and ends, donned my freshly washed clothes, and went down to the checkout desk to discuss the bill. I explained that I was a budget traveler with very little money, but that we could contact my parents in Scotland and settle the account with their help. When I asked about the amount of the bill, I was completely surprised by their magnanimous response: *There is no bill. We take care of those who visit us.*

I was astonished. These hospitable, generous people had gone to very considerable lengths to restore my health. They had basically saved my life, and were not asking for a single toman. If something like this had happened in America, I could well have been presented with a bill for six figures, and I might have been in debt for the rest of my days trying to repay it.

So I do think about health matters when I am traveling, but I don't worry about these things unduly. Although I have never had to use it yet, I usually take out some basic travel insurance and carry on from there.

Tie the camel, and leave the rest to Allah, as a vintage proverb goes. Because, if something untoward did befall me in the friendly, developing countries I enjoy exploring, it would most likely not result in the kind of life-derailing financial disaster that this type of event might turn into in America. But let us not misconstrue things here. Medical care in America can certainly be exorbitant for the uninsured, but it is also almost always of a high standard. Medical care in some of these lands of the East may be far less expensive or even free, but all is not sweetness and light either. Some aspects of it can be positively appalling.

For instance, during one of several tours of Pakistan there was a major outbreak of yellow fever. Outbreaks like this are fairly common there, especially during the summer monsoon times. The extreme heat, the consistently wet conditions, and the overflowing sewers and drains trigger an exuberant carnival of microbes and germs. Even though this particular outbreak did not become an international epidemic, it was sufficiently widespread to alarm Pakistan's neighbors. These countries promptly stipulated that everyone now coming into their territory from Pakistan had to have an official stamp in their passport showing that they had been vaccinated against the disease. This regulation affected me directly. My visa, along with that of a fellow tourist from Italy, was just about to expire. We were planning to travel from Karachi to Kabul to get them renewed that same week. We had to get these stamps right away.

We tracked down the name and location of the official vaccinating hospital, and hailed a taxi to take us there. Given the huge size and the legendary congestion of the city, we were expecting this to turn into a strenuous quest. We were not disappointed. When we pulled up in front of the hospital, we thought we must have come to the wrong address. It didn't look or feel right at all. The place was absolutely immense, one of the largest buildings I have ever seen. There were weeds and rubbish all over the grounds, the windows were encrusted with a thick layer of soot-like grit, and there did not appear to be anyone around. When we made our way rather tentatively inside, our misgivings increased. There was no one on duty, no signs, no waiting areas, no nurses, no reception desks, nothing at all except endless, unswept space. It looked and felt like an abandoned airport terminal.

However, our resourceful taxi driver cum chief translator rose to the occasion. He went around knocking on various doors, and eventually found someone in an obscure office some way off to one side of the main entrance. He made appropriate enquiries, and returned with directions for where we were supposed to go. We set off down one of the cavernous, empty halls, and, after a lengthy tramp, arrived at the room that he had been sent to. Bicycles would not have been out of place for getting around in these seemingly endless passageways.

The vaccination room was spartan in the extreme. All it contained was a battered metal desk and a few uncomfortable folding chairs. With considerable unease, we sat down on the rigid chairs and waited.

About fifteen minutes later, someone I thought was probably the janitor came in and started poking around by the desk. As it turned out, this was in fact the doctor in charge of vaccinations. From a top drawer he produced a hefty, old-fashioned, glass syringe nearly three quarters of an inch in diameter, and about six inches long. He then took out a hair-raisingly large, thick needle and slowly screwed it on to the end of the syringe. It was so big we could clearly see the hole at the tip of it from the other side of the desk. We were looking at some sort of horse needle here.

In one of the bottom drawers he located an unmarked mason jar containing about a pint of murky liquid that looked a lot like dishwater. Now in my experience, medicines for injections are kept in refrigerators, and they come in small vials plastered with multiple labels that contain expiration dates, instructions for proper storage, directions about the dosages, and so forth. They also have a rubber seal in the middle of the cap where the needle is inserted to extract the liquid into the syringe in a sterile manner. This jar had none of these things: no labels, no dates, no instructions, no rubber seal. The doctor was simply going to remove the lid, lower the needle into the dishwater, and pull out whatever dose he thought was fit. As you can probably imagine, we sat there watching with rising alarm. While he was focusing on getting this stuff ready, we quietly stepped into the hallway, exchanged looks of mutual panic, and took off. Even the driver agreed that this operation was just too dodgy to mess with.

A short time later, catching our breath back at the car, we were unsure what to do next. We had narrowly avoided the medical Middle Ages inside, but we still needed to get the stamps in order to leave the country. We were seriously stuck. At this point, our heaven-sent taxi driver told us that if we gave him our passports, and fifty rupees, he would go get the stamps and return in the evening. He didn't provide any details as to what sort of shady, back-room deal he had in mind, and we didn't press him. But, after a brief round of deliberation, that's what we did. We handed him the money and our documents, and then we went home and waited. True to his word, about sundown he brought them back with official stamps duly and neatly affixed. We were now good to go.

To this day, I am thoroughly amazed that we actually did this. Nowadays I wouldn't dream of handing my passport to a rank stranger, especially in Karachi, of all places. But, hey, it worked. We set out on the long grind up to the Khyber Pass, and crossed the Afghan border without mishap a few days later. Sometimes being young and foolish can be an advantage.

Having said that, I do think there are people walking up here who would do well to be more thoughtful and cautious about their health. A few years ago, I met a Scottish gentleman heading up towards the Mt. Everest region wearing a hunting vest on top of his down jacket. All of the pockets of this vest were packed with little airplane-sized bottles of whisky. He was sipping his way up to base camp, moving at high speed, and humming catchy Scottish ballads the while. Even his guide couldn't keep up with him. The guide was a day or two behind.

Guide's bloody knackered, he explained. His theory was that if you drank enough firewater and went up and then right back down again fast enough, the effects of high altitude and bacteria would not have a chance to catch up with you. I have never actually tried this procedure myself. However, all things considered, I probably wouldn't recommend this approach.

Another time, some of us were hanging around the lodge one evening sipping mugs of hot tea and brandy. Sitting close to us by the stove there was a Russian tourist who was describing his forthcoming schedule. His plan was to go straight up to Everest Base Camp, which is well over five thousand meters, and then climb a nearby peak that was over six thousand meters, all within the next few days, with no thought of pausing or slowing down to get used to those elevations at all. When he had finished mapping out this brash vision, we asked him with some concern if he was worried about getting AMS.

Oh, no. Life is short, he insisted. Indeed.

I am also rather dumbfounded by the way some people eat on these trails. I have a friend from the Appalachian region of western North Carolina who often comes to Nepal to walk. He can't get enough of the high mountain landscapes here. He also can't get enough of the national cuisine. As soon as he is on the trail, all caution about food is thrown to the winds. While I am sitting there hesitantly picking at my plain rice and boiled eggs, he tucks into the popular local dishes with lip-smacking abandon, and then calls for a second round. And every time, every single time, he goes home with a lingering, gut-wrenching dose of giardia. I think he is probably the unofficial king of giardia, as a matter of fact.

However, it is not difficult to see how caution about food falls by the wayside. It happens like this. You get up and start walking early in the morning, and by the time you get to your hotel sometime in the late afternoon, you are 'bloody knackered' and very hungry. You sit down at a table in the dining room and open the menu. There in front of you are several pages of photographs showing all of the delectable possibilities. You browse with deep interest and attention through the soup section, the assorted fried rice options, the pizzas, and the spaghettis. And then your gaze falls on a sumptuous burger presented with a grand stack of fries. You think: *Yes-sir-eee! Just what the doctor ordered. I'll have one of these, please.*

It comes to your table. You wolf it down in rapturous, half-chewed bliss, and retire to your room and get into your sleeping bag feeling warm and complete and deeply content. And then, somewhere in the early hours, the rumblings within begin, and by sunrise you are basically living in the bathroom, gushing from both ends, deep content long gone. Not the doctor's recommendation at all, it turns out.

In fine, you do need to be careful when you are traveling like this. However, you need not worry too much about avalanches sweeping you away in the dead of night, or about rakshi-crazed ax murderers lurking with intent around the next bend, or about lumbering yaks shouldering you off a precipice into the abyss, and so forth. But beware the siren call of the burger of death that comes in an unthinking moment of fatigue and bodily need.

18

O true apothecary, thy drugs are quick.

William Shakespeare

The plan today was to walk out of the side valley of Lake Tilicho and return to the Annapurna Circuit route leading up towards the pass a few days farther along. The narrow trail meandered its way through flourishing meadows of bedewed grass, past some primitive shepherds' encampments, and then over a high ridge affording a wide view of the whole area and the distant summits far above. The top of the ridge was decorated with a bleached yak skull with long, curved horns carefully placed on a tall cairn, beneath the customary, multi-colored strings of shuddering prayer flags. I paused here to catch my breath and to absorb the lay of the land. The fine view from up there was the most map-like, comprehensive vista of the area I had seen yet. This eagle's perch was followed by a long, awkward descent that was quite hard on the knees. Coming down that stretch, I decided that you really do need to have two trekking poles to descend on this type of breakneck terrain safely, and added them to the *must get when back in town* shopping list.

I was now following the main AC valley once again up towards its starting point well above the timber line. The path went through fields dotted here and there with the small stone houses of the local villagers, and many large boulders dislodged from the cliffs above long ago. This was exactly the sort of open, high alpine walking I enjoy most and had come here hoping to find. This section also contained one of the cleanest and most welcoming tea shops on the entire circuit, surrounded by some pretty aspen trees, leaves a-shiver in the rising afternoon breeze. This neat establishment was operated by a particularly polite and courteous manager. It was in this place that I discovered another dependable and most welcome addition to my sparse diet: coconut-filled chocolate bars. These power-packed delectations really do put some wings on your feet, especially when they are washed down with large cups of steaming milk tea. Katia, a school teacher from Moscow, bumped into me here. After a leisurely, introductory break at this tea stand, we strolled on from there together for several more hours, chatting, and wending our way up the path to the minimal rest houses of Ledar.

Our hotel in Ledar was still under construction. The room had recently been painted, apparently just before we arrived, and it reeked strongly of fresh paint. I became rather dizzy and nauseous from the fumes while I was taking a rest in there. At first, I thought that the mountain sickness symptoms I had experienced up near Lake Tilicho were coming back, but these went away when I came out to attend the cocktail hour a short time later. A little hot rum mixed with cloves and honey is very restorative at the end of a long day climbing steep hills in the rain.

The water system for the lodge was not installed yet either. The only water on hand was from a hose lying on the ground out in the yard behind the building. To make use of this, you had to pull the two halves of the hose apart at a plastic joint in the middle, and then endeavor to reconnect them when you were done. This proved to be a rather finicky operation, and I got nicely soaked attempting it. Life really is fraught with peril and inconvenience.

Over in the dining room we met Soo Yun, an especially stylish and smartly dressed Korean girl who was walking the circuit with a Nepali guide. She was the quintessential picture of an outdoor-wear model. She had on a floppy, rainbow-striped, knitted wool hat, a tastefully arranged Kashmiri scarf, a top-of-the-line, turquoise windbreaker that fit her to perfection, equally made to order, navy-blue waterproofs, and dayglow yellow trainers. She was probably the most elegant fashion statement I have ever beheld on a trail.

However, Soo Yun was not feeling anywhere near as good as she looked. She was very much under the weather with some major altitude problems that appeared to be getting dangerous. She was quite sick and thoroughly disheartened, leaning dejectedly on her table, and was on the verge of abandoning her walk. Fortunately, I had lots of Diamox tablets with me, far more than I needed, and gave her a handful. She took one, and what a change it made. Within an hour or two she was significantly better, cheerfully eating dinner with a solid appetite, and showering me with heartfelt gratitude in the effusive Asian manner. The whole house, especially her worried guide, was cheered to see this rapid and surprising recovery.

I bumped into Soo Yun again a few days later just below the pass, slowly but bravely ascending. I do believe she made it up and over the top. Diamox can really make a difference. One should not go walking in the Himalayas without it.

19

*The finest landscape in the world is improved
by a good inn in the foreground.*

Samuel Johnson (attributed)

The most elevated section of the Annapurna Circuit begins after Ledar. In this region you are well above the forest, walking on barren, rocky hillsides beneath long, steep slopes of rough, beige-colored shingle and sharp, snow-clad ridges. It is a starkly beautiful zone in spite of the increasingly sparse vegetation. I continued on along the rocky path to the cliff-bound village of Phedi, which I reached at about twelve o'clock. Katia, a very early riser, had arrived there several hours before me. In Nepali, *Phedi* means something like 'bottom of the pass', somewhat similar to *pied du port* in Saint-Jean-Pied-de-Port at the start of the Camino Frances in the Pyrenees. Many of the major passes in Nepal have villages called Phedi just below them. These small habitations are often the starting point for pass crossings.

This one was a disappointment. The only lodges open were dirty and unswept, the dining rooms were cluttered with unwashed dishes and general disarray, and the beds were unmade. In my experience, with few exceptions, the best places to stay in these small, mountain villages are almost always guest houses that are in the very competent hands of Nepali women, as I have carefully explained to my guides on several occasions. Inns like that just aren't in the same class as those that are being operated by *I wish I were somewhere else* teenagers. The lodges run by mountain women are clean and well-managed, and they are nicely decorated with heirlooms, family photographs, numerous pots of flowers, and brightly polished copper vessels hanging from the walls. They also have cheerful rooms, washed curtains, pretty gardens, and excellent food. However, guest houses of that type did not seem to be available in Phedi during this low tourist season.

Katia and I decided to push on to Thorung High Camp, a small group of buildings at the top of an almost vertical, four-hundred-meter ascent farther up towards the pass. This steep climb turned out to be a lot less difficult than it looked. Thorough acclimatization had been a long time coming, but was finally starting to kick in.

High Camp was a far more welcoming and encouraging place than Phedi. There was only one basic hotel set in some small stony fields, but it was much more organized than those we had seen just below. A heavy rain began falling as we arrived. We narrowly missed a chilling soaking that would have caught us if we had come several minutes later. Even though this was mid-summer, it was quite cold at this height, still some degrees above freezing, but very wintery nonetheless. The heavy-duty, Merino wool, long underwear I had found on clearance in Vermont a few months earlier was a major windfall. We went to our rooms and jumped into our sleeping bags. The rain continued all afternoon, during which some forlorn-looking horses wearing delightfully tuneful, musical bells wandered in and out of the prevailing fog outside, sending lovely, pure notes floating through the mist.

Getting on towards sundown I climbed out of

my warm, dry bed and sloshed over to the dining room to get something to eat. (How did travelers in former centuries ever go anywhere without 800 fill down?) While I was waiting for my usual conservative and not very imaginative menu selections to arrive, I picked up a month-old English newspaper from Kathmandu that was lying on a bench near me. I was absent-mindedly browsing through it, looking at some of the pictures and the headlines, and glancing at the comics in dentist waiting room mode, when a letter to the editor caught my eye. Its non-native writer was addressing the government of Nepal, stridently insisting that phone towers should be installed on all of the main passes in the country right away to make posting selfies faster and more convenient, how indecent it was to keep friends and followers waiting, etc., etc.

The language and the tone of this letter were completely over the top. The author was not suggesting, not recommending, not requesting, not appealing, but rudely and arrogantly demanding that this absolute and blatantly obvious necessity be attended to immediately. This person was angry and offended by such a reprehensible and egregious omission on the part of the government. I was truly taken aback. Not to harp on this topic, but incidents such as these keep on coming. The untarnished alpine meadows and boulder fields surrounding the high passes of the Himalayas are among the most magical places still left on Earth. These gems should be trashed to enable some narcissistic moron to broadcast himself marginally faster? Am I missing something here? I mean, what is going on with these people?

If I had to take a guess at it, I think we are witnessing another case in which technology is affecting the ways in which humans view the world and conduct themselves in it, as it often has done historically. For example, take the humble bicycle. Before the bicycle was invented, rural folks who were looking for mates went a-courting within a radius of where they lived based on how far they could walk on their day off. When bicycles came along, this situation changed. With bicycles, they could socialize over a much wider area based on the distance they could ride in a day. This had some significant effects on social expectations and attitudes, marriage patterns, shopping habits, and the gene pool, among other things. I think something of this sort may be happening again with mobile technology, especially for many younger people who have never known a world without it. It looks to me like humanity is currently undergoing a major cultural shift into a more self-obsessed perception of the world than has previously obtained. This is swiftly becoming more and more evident across a wide range of behaviors and social norms.

As I am an English teacher, English teacherly illustrations tend to suggest themselves, please to bear with me. Consider popular literature as a reflection of cultural standards and an indicator of societal change. Take a look at an adventure travel book that was published and widely read about the beginning of the twentieth century. This book is *Sailing Alone Around the World* by Captain Joshua Slocum from New England. In the 1890s, Captain Slocum spent three years circumnavigating the planet in *Spray*, a thirty-six-foot wooden sloop that had no engine, no electricity, no radio, no GPS, no locator beacon, no microwave, and no refrigeration, not to mention no antibiotics and no ibuprofen. He was the first person to sail all the way around the world alone.

This was a remarkable and highly original achievement that had attracted much of the world's interest, and his book quickly became a best seller. Not surprisingly, writing styles vary a great deal from one writer to another. They also vary quite a lot from one era to another, reflecting the zeitgeist of their times. As such, *Sailing Alone Around the*

World embodies the tone and the norms of the late nineteenth century. When Captain Slocum presents this history-making voyage, the camera is seldom focused on himself. If he is in the frame at all, he is usually just a small figure down in the bottom corner, humbly and skillfully directing the reader's attention outward to the action and the grandeur beyond him.

When Slocum was weighing which route to follow on his journey around the world, he was advised by seasoned naval captains to risk the ferocious storms surrounding Cape Horn rather than the murderous pirates operating near the Bab-al-Mandeb (the Gate of Tears) at the southern entrance to the Red Sea. As a result, some months later he found himself struggling to claw his way through the foggy, gale-prone Straits of Magellan into the Pacific in conditions that were especially dangerous and severe for small sailboats. This took several weeks and involved a number of attempts, as he cautiously and doggedly steered his little vessel through the extreme winds and the monstrous waves of Patagonia, which could easily have smashed his boat and killed him. His words:

> …on the morning of March 4, the wind shifted to southwest, and then back suddenly to northwest, and blew with terrific force. The

Spray, stripped of her sails, then bore off under bare poles. No ship in the world could have stood up against so violent a gale... The first day of the storm gave the Spray her actual test in the worst sea that Cape Horn or its wild regions could afford, and in no part of the world could a rougher sea be found... There the Spray rode, now like a bird on the crest of a wave, and now like a waif deep down in the hollow between seas, and so she drove on...

> Captain Joshua Slocum

On his final attempt, Slocum ventured out from the straits and stood at the wheel for thirty hours until *Spray* was properly underway in the Southern Ocean beyond the savage winds and the massive waves battering the Chilean coast. This ordeal demanded a great deal of skill, and hour upon hour of unwavering courage and grit. This singlehanded passage under sail alone was one of the most difficult and dangerous feats of seamanship ever recorded, beyond exceptional, bordering on the miraculous. However, you have to read fairly carefully between the lines to understand just how daunting it actually was. He describes this in language notable for its simple modesty and strikingly unassuming understatement. Even in truly heroic moments like these, he does not draw attention to himself. Captain Slocum was not carrying a selfie stick.

Most citizens of the twenty-first century just don't have this kind of self-effacing perspective and vocabulary any more. Instead, with the 'new normal' that is so aggressively asserting itself in our time, we seem to be drifting into an ever more self-absorbed state. I think the current global epidemic of universal mobile phone addiction is both a symptom and a contributing factor. And that is probably enough of a rant for this chapter.

20

May all living things be happy.

Prayer flag

We were back on the trail at first light, and reached the top of the pass about mid-morning. With an elevation well over five thousand meters, Thorung La is the highest point on the Annapurna Circuit. This area is definitely one of the grandest and most scenic places I have ever visited. Thorung La has been called the largest pass on Earth, and it could well be, from the look of it, being considerably wider than the other passes I have crossed. It is surrounded by towering, icy cliffs crowned with broad expanses of the untrodden snows drifting in and out of wafting fogs and watery sun. Strong winds and clouds drive continually between these stark, sheer walls, griffons and lammergeiers float serenely overhead, and echoing boulders rumble down long rocky slopes in the background.

This is the classic, storybook Himalayan pass, like something you would really expect to see on an expedition to discover Shangri-La. Both sides overlook nearly endless vistas of range upon range of lofty, distant mountains. To the north-west, your eyes sweep over the alpine deserts of Mustang and on into Tibet, and to the east are the snow-wrapped peaks of Manaslu, the Ganesh Himal, and the Langtang region. For us non-climbing types, a place like this really is the roof of the world. If you happen to be considering travel plans, Thorung La makes a noble and uplifting destination.

I sat there on the stones with cartloads of multihued prayer flags fluttering above me, waiting for my Russian trail buddy to come up. I now had a decision to make. I was trying to choose between continuing westwards with her down to the ancient pilgrim center of Muktinath, and onward from there to Jomsom, and eventually Pokhara far below, or remaining on the eastern slope and returning to Besi

Sahar through the Marsyangdi valley I had ascended.

I was reluctant to continue over the pass for a number of reasons. Muktinath, the next stopping place that had suitable guest houses and shops, was about nine kilometers away. The Annapurna Circuit loses almost two vertical kilometers within that distance, from about five and a half thousand meters down to something a bit over three and a half. This makes for a long, steep descent that can be rough on the joints, which were already swollen and hurting. On this day, that side was covered in thick clouds right up to the level of the pass. This jarring descent would have to be made in a cold, dense fog with almost no visibility. In addition, I had already walked the Jomsom valley trails several times before this. It was not new ground for me.

That part of the Annapurna Circuit is also considerably busier than the Manang side. There are military installations and an active airport, along with a number of hydro-electric projects and extensive power lines. There is more construction and infrastructure, and the road down to Pokhara now has considerably more traffic on it than the basic track on the eastern side. In addition to more traffic, that part of the road is also beset with frequent landslides and rock falls during the summer monsoon season. The day before this one, the circuit grapevine had brought news that a British tourist had been killed over there by a falling stone. Heart-in-your-mouth horror stories of bus and jeep wheels mere inches from sudden-death precipices abound as well. The Jomsom road is not recommended for the faint of heart.

After weighing all this, I decided it would probably be better to return on the side I had come up. The Manang area is not only quieter and simpler and more culturally intact than the Jomsom side, it is also greener, and the Nepalese government has opened new routes farther down to bring walkers away from the road. In addition, there were a number of alternative high routes there that I had not yet been on.

Katia arrived about that time and plied me with mixed nuts and raisins. Then a thick fog pushed through the pass, the views vanished, and the temperature began to plummet. It was time to leave. Before we parted, I arranged to meet up with Katia back in Kathmandu after the walk. She told me to expect her with a freshly shaved head (she didn't say anything about the eyebrows), and then she disappeared into the clouds over to the left. I dallied a few moments, wondering if I would ever stand there again, and then started down into the mists swirling up on the right.

The descent back to High Camp, following the path through the thick, shifting fogs at a leisurely and careful pace, took me several hours. Having pretty well exhausted the sights there and in Phedi just below it, I decided to continue on down and connect with some of the trails I had not been on. This was going to be a race, as the two o'clock rains were about to start. A race that I lost, in the event. I was soon caught in yet another sweeping rainstorm, which brought out the sturdy, green umbrella once again. Apropos of which, I much prefer to walk under an umbrella instead of being shrouded inside a poncho. You can see a lot better, for one thing, and you are free from that noisy, claustrophobic hood, for another.

The terrain around Thorung La is the most striking and dramatic landscape that you encounter along the Annapurna Circuit. The harsh beauties of the tremendous slopes and the faraway horizons awaken a strong sense of life as an epic journey. However, this region can also be deadly. Every year, a number of visitors misjudge its dangers and die up here. They don't understand how abruptly and how severely these heights can affect you, out of the blue, as it were.

One evening, on another trail over in the Everest region, I met a Chinese girl in a guest house situated at about four and a half thousand meters. By then I had significantly exceeded the five-hundred-meters-a-day ascent limit, and I was starting to feel rather shaky and unwell. It was clear that I needed to stay put for a day or so before proceeding any farther. I took out my book and settled in next to the wood stove for the long haul. This Chinese girl, on the other hand, was feeling good and fit, and she departed cheerfully after a hearty breakfast the next morning. However, around lunchtime she arrived at another village that was only a few hundred meters higher up, desperately ill, and was taken out in a helicopter a short time later. Somewhere in the midst of that moderate ascent, she had crossed a personal tipping point. A few extra meters can have a major impact.

Another day I joined a crew of Belgians who had just arrived at a comparable elevation about three o'clock in the afternoon. At this point they were all feeling fine and normal, and they sat down to a late lunch with robust appetites and lots of lively banter and upbeat jokes (politely and fluently told in English for my sake). But then, sometime during the night, one member of the group completely fell apart within the space of only a few hours. At first light, her rescue helicopter landed on the grass outside the hotel, thoroughly scaring the poor yaks that were standing there next to the wall. She looked terrible, and was lucky that the weather had allowed the helicopter to land. These on-call helicopter services are a fairly new development in some of the higher areas. Only a few years prior to this, she would probably have had to stumble down the mountain path for hours to get to a more amenable level or an HRA (Himalayan Rescue Association) aid post, quite possibly at night with only a head lamp, which would have been no fun at all.

These rescue helicopters bring out quite a roster of people who might not survive otherwise. But sometimes they can't make it in, and then things can quickly become dire. When I was up here another time during the winter, a traveler from Australia came down with serious altitude symptoms just as a major Himalayan blizzard was beginning. Helicopters couldn't fly in those conditions, and by the time the storm had abated about thirty-six hours later, he was dead. He went out on a helicopter in a body bag. These types of things most commonly happen when unacclimated visitors try to fit what they view as the journey of a lifetime into too short a time frame. They ascend too fast. While I am not trying to suggest that the visitors are dropping like flies here, the potential hazards of this kind of high-altitude walking should not be underestimated.

In addition, the perils of these upper regions are not limited to AMS. Another afternoon on that winter trip, a couple of tourists and their guide arrived at a picturesque stopover next to a frozen, alpine lake. They left their packs in the hotel and headed out to take a few photographs of the snowy mountain scene. Unbeknownst to them, there was a layer of smooth ice under snow on the steep shores of the lake. When they stepped on this, they lost their footing, slid down to the lake, and crashed through the ice into the frigid water below. The local people saw this happen from the other side of the lake, and got to them as soon as they could. However, it was so cold (January, the roof of the world, late afternoon, very windy) advanced hypothermia rapidly overtook them, and all three of them were dead a short time later. This zone is truly beautiful, but you do have to be careful up there.

Incidentally, there is other stuff you need to be watchful about in the high country besides just your physical well-being. Another recent development that appeared with the advent of these private helicopter companies is a new scam. Nowadays some unscrupulous guides make their trusting and inexperienced clients ascend much too quickly on purpose. They are trying to ensure that AMS will result, and that an expensive helicopter rescue will thereby become necessary, for which the guide will then be paid a handsome commission. Who thinks this stuff up? It is remarkable how closely the scams keep pace with the advances in technology.

21

Now comes the mystery.

Henry Ward Beecher

Unlike some of the other recent mornings, this one dawned clear and bright. The sky was cloudless and deep blue, and the air was chilly and breezy. The trail here was moderate and mostly flat, passing through expansive grazing pastures larded with bedazzling alpine flowers and the occasional romping baby yak. It was a perfect walking day. It was also a perfect drying day for the local people. Almost all of the villagers I passed by were taking advantage of this break in the weather to air things out. The grass in front of their small stone houses was covered with bamboo trays full of mushrooms and herbs they'd gathered on the slopes above, plastic tarps spread with barley grains and potatoes, and all manner and sizes of laundry, drying in the morning sun.

As I ambled downhill on the easy path with a light heart, the vision of Manang waxed ever rosier in my mind's eye: bona fide hot showers; clean kitchens serving some of the best food on the whole circuit; modern washing machines that really worked; well-stocked shops abounding. After the likes of Phedi and Ledar, Manang was positively downtown, a rollicking outbreak of luxury and extravagance. It was time for a proper cleanup and some serious refurbishing after the hardships and privations of the pass. There is nothing like a day of rest in a town after a long turn of slogging the muddy trail in thin air.

Around noon I stopped at a small cluster of farm houses named Ghunsang for a short break and cup of pace-quickening hot lemonade. I parked myself at a handy picnic table by a pretty lodge and admired its burgeoning garden while the lemonade was a-making. This tidy spread contained many of the usual local suspects: long beds of sturdy daisies in several colors, walls of tall hollyhocks, lines of cooking-book-perfect cabbages and spinach, and, not surprisingly, numerous specimens of the ubiquitous, irrepressible ganja. I think they really do plant themselves.

In the midst of this botanizing, the French co-manager and friend of the hotel owner brought out the drink and sat down at the table. We fell to chatting, and she told me that a Yeti had recently been sighted next to a small lake that I passed on the way in. And, it had not been just one Yeti. There had been two of them. An adult was seen playing with a youngster at the water's edge. She told me that even though the local people were normally somewhat guarded about discussing this subject, this was actually a true report. (According to local tradition, Yetis are seen as harbingers of misfortune; such sightings can herald trouble and bad luck for whole villages.)

I am not sure what to think about this Yeti stuff. Like many of us, I am not really a true believer. Almost all of the so-called 'evidence' that has been collected over the years has turned out to be either completely false or seriously misleading. There have been outright hoaxers filming themselves slinking about the forest in the Pacific Northwest in shaggy monkey costumes. There are numerous photographs of unusually large footprints found in the snow that turned out to be melting bear tracks. And there are deeply venerated, mysterious scalps moldering away in the cabinets of ancient monasteries that most probably also belonged to bears, or possibly to Himalayan mountain goats. In view of these kinds of things, by and large I am usually a Yeti skeptic.

But not completely. Some of the evidence out there is not as easy to just dismiss out of hand. A number of articulate and well-educated people have reported a range of far more plausible signs. Some of the plaster molds taken from huge footprints left in the mud have been well documented. Some of these footprints don't look like bear tracks at all. They are very humanlike, with distinct arches, clear-cut toes, and no claw marks.

In addition, I recently looked at a well-made documentary on TV that was seriously believable. This highly tenable account was presented by some fishermen who had a camp on a remote lake in northern Canada that was accessible only by planes able to land on water. One year, after they had gone home for the winter, something big broke into their cabin and thoroughly trashed it. This area was too distant for young vandals to frequent, and other fishermen generally don't do that sort of thing. Ravenous bears, however, frequently break into isolated huts searching for food, so they assumed that the damage must have been caused by a marauding bear. They cleaned up the mess and repaired the cabin. And before they left the camp for that season, they took measures to prevent a repeat performance. They assembled several pieces of heavy plywood, pounded lots of long, thick nails through them, and then secured these boards in front of the door and under the windows.

A few nights before they left the camp, something hung around out in the trees nearby, and threw a series of large rocks onto the roof over the course of several hours. Although this rock-throwing happened two or three nights in succession, they couldn't figure out who or what was doing it. After they had gone away, something did try to break in again, but was apparently put off by the new, heavily spiked doormats that were now in place. Whatever it was, it stepped on some of the nails and then ran off. However, while doing this, it left some blood and bits of tissue behind, which were sent to a laboratory for DNA analysis. The results were surprising. According to the lab report, the material left on the nails did not come from a bear. It was primate DNA.

This documentary was made by seemingly truthful, responsible citizens. Evidence like this could suggest that there might actually be something still unknown living in remote areas like this one. It does not seem very likely that someone would go to all the trouble of flying bits of monkey (or a whole one) far into the wilderness just to substantiate a hoax or to play a joke on their friends. If there is something like a Yeti, it would most probably be a highly endangered species now on the edge of extinction. This could explain why credible sightings are so rare. But who knows, in centuries past, before we humans became so efficient and mechanical and zealous about slashing and burning Planet Earth, there may have been more of these shy, elusive creatures around, and hence all the similar descriptions and legends scattered throughout the world. All things considered, on most days I remain pretty much of a skeptic. Nonetheless, part of me would like to believe that the Yeti really is out there, laying low somewhere deep in the woods.

22

Hey diddle dumpling, my son John,
One shoe off, and one shoe on.

Nursery rhyme

After a good bath, several leisurely visits to the dining room, and a day off the feet, I set out once again on the long traverse from Manang to Lower Pisang, about a day's journey farther down the valley. The sky was nicely overcast, with a hint of rain. These are the sort of conditions I hope for when I am doing longer stages. Except at very high altitudes, I rather dread the parting of the clouds. Fortunately, this usually does not happen for long during the monsoon.

However, even though the day was very congenial, and the occasional views were sublime and grand, my attention was not on the skyscraping scenery. I was having painful trouble with my shoes yet once again. You would think, that after all of the long-distance walking I have done, with the thousands of kilometers I have covered, and the extravagant collection of shoes and socks I have gone through over the years, that I would have learned how to select a suitable pair of boots by this time. Alas, this has not been the case.

When I first started hiking about twenty years ago on the trails of Mt. Katahdin in Maine, I made a mistake that quite a few new walkers make. I bought some hiking boots that were the same size as my normal shoes. They felt fine in the store, but out on the trail they soon produced all manner of discomfort as my feet swelled and my toes started bashing into the front of the boots. After a few weeks of this, I upgraded to a size larger, but that didn't really solve the problem. The same troubles still continued at a slightly reduced level of intensity. Then I tried walking in boots that were two full sizes larger than my everyday street shoes. This was a major improvement; progress was being made. However, on multi-week adventures, especially on routes that involved the carrying of a large pack such as the Appalachian Trail and the Pacific Crest, my feet soon swelled so much that even these, which had seemed so hugely over-sized when I was stomping around in the store, once again turned out to be too small for sustained use on longer journeys.

However, I think there may have been a real breakthrough here, at long last. Recently, while following the Camino Frances in northern Spain, I came across a pair of size US fifteen walking shoes in a small hiking shop just down the street from the Cathedral of Santa Maria in central Pamplona. Some of you pilgrims may know of it. This was really unusual. Anything in size fifteen is very hard to find, even in stores in America. Sizes like that usually have to be specially ordered, or even custom-made. And here they were just sitting there on the shelf along with all of the other more common sizes. These shoes had it all: enough room in the front to accommodate seriously swollen feet, excellent arch support, and a proper fit in the heel. Karma works in mysterious ways.

I think I may finally be getting the right idea of the thing. Let's say your normal shoe size is a twelve (like mine). To walk comfortably for several weeks or more, you need to put some decent, shock absorbing insoles into your boots to cushion your knees. These do not have to be especially bulky or super high-tech. The types of shoe inserts that are commonly available in most drugstores will do fine. To make room for this insole, you will probably need to include an extra size, especially if the new insole you select is thicker than the original one. And, for the long-term well-being of your feet, you should be wearing a sock made of good quality wool or the equivalent. Again, this sock does not have to be super-thick or heavy-duty. A medium Merino wool hiking sock should be good. Allowing enough room for this sock might also require adding on another size. And lastly, you have to leave some extra space up in the front to handle the swelling that will surely result when you walk for a long time with a large load. This could require the addition of another size as well, which brings us to the following guidelines:

your normal shoe size	( )
room for a good insole	(+1)
room for a decent sock	(+1)
room for foot swelling	(+1)
CLD:(comfortable long-distance size)	( )

In my case, this would be 12 + 1 + 1 + 1 = 15.

I have stepped out of sports stores the world over carrying newly purchased walking shoes, brimming with hope that this pair, yea, these very ones right here in this box, were indeed, at last, the right size. This has included at least half a dozen size fourteens. But in the end, almost all of them have proved to be unsuitable when they were actually tested in the field. The blisters, the bunions, the swelling, and the lost toenails have continued apace, in spite of many types and combinations of socks, and stacks of medical tape. The one exception was this pair I discovered in Pamplona, which, it turned out, happened to be in line with the specs listed in the table above. I really do wonder if modern boot makers base their shoe size claims on the length of the outside sole instead of on the actual interior volume.

The next time I visit my storage unit in New England, I am going to round up my entire supply of crippling footwear, cart the lot over to Goodwill, and start anew. Henceforth I am not stepping out the door on a long trip in anything less than a size US fifteen. I realize that this is bordering on the clown shoe zone, but I have had enough mangled feet for several walking careers already. I am sure that other folks have had more success in finding suitable shoes that fit nicely without having to go to clown sizes, but thus far, this hasn't worked out very well for me.

23

*This is the forest primeval,
The murmuring pines and the hemlocks
stand like Druids of old…*

Henry Wadsworth Longfellow

For the last several weeks, the route had been passing through the alpine grasses and the stony tracts of the arid regions well above the trees. On this section between Pisang and Chame, it dropped back into the resin-scented forest. I was away early on a tiny path through the fields of vividly blooming buckwheat heading down towards the pines. Yesterday I must have wished for gray skies just a little too fervently.

The clouds thickened and heavy rain began to fall soon after I set out. *Be careful what you wish for* would be the well-worn but appropriate byword for this cold, soaking morning. Incidentally, I am not really a weather fanatic, or even that much of an enthusiast, actually. It's just that when you walk like this, the weather conditions you're facing are really critical, so you notice and think about them more than you may do back in civilian life spent largely indoors and getting about by car. When you rise in the morning, this is the first thing you look to. That is why so many of these weather references find their way into my notes.

After carrying on alone for a spell, I was overtaken by a large gang of noisy Indian teenagers. It was remarkable just how much of a ruckus this crowd was managing to generate. They were chattering away non-stop, whacking rocks and trees with their trekking poles, accosting their mates ahead and behind, and yes, you guessed it, blasting several kinds of screechy pop music as they went. This crew was quite spread out, and most of them were about fifty years younger than me. Trying to outwalk them would have required a sustained, focused effort. I was stuck in a traveling bubble of continuous racket. Fortunately, a large open pickup truck was waiting for them at a tea house on the side of the track a few kilometers farther on, and the whole clamorous procession climbed into the back, whooping loudly, and shouting out the usual sort of mindless nonsense beloved by teenagers the world over.

When the rowdies had gone, the forest was very different. It was now full of sounds of another sort: the rain falling on the pine needles and the leaves; the wind whispering through the branches; the voice of the river, like distant surf somewhere out of sight far below, punctuated now and again with the sharp cries of birds and the mellifluous pinging of horse bells drifting through the trees. After almost an hour walking along listening to this second chorus, I caught up with the pickup truck and the dinful teenagers once again, completely stuck in the deep mud, bemired to the axles. A valiant digging-out operation was underway in the rain. It looked like this was going to be a long, soggy job. Motoring in the Himalayas during the rainy season does have its limitations.

I arrived in Chame about mid-afternoon, took another room at the Marsyangdi Guest House, and gladly put down the dripping pack. I did a few errands around the shopping areas, and then retired to my room for a bit of pre-dinner chill out. During the monsoon season many of the hotels in the hills are a little on the clammy side because of the height and all the moisture in the air. To counter this, I brought out my brass, elephant-shaped incense burner, placed a stick of jasmine incense into the hole in its back, and put a match to it, which quickly freshened up the place considerably. Then I poured myself a glass of whisky to warm up the rain-chilled innards a notch as well.

My attention must have been drifting somewhere else, because I accidently spilled a fair slug of this on the dark wooden floorboards. I quickly grabbed a baby-wipe from the night stand and mopped up the spilled whisky with that. And then, in the spirit of *waste not*, I washed my feet with it, producing what were undoubtedly the most aromatic feet I have ever had in all my travels. There really is a first time for just about everything, it would seem. Incidentally, what an outstanding, multi-purpose, always useful invention baby-wipes are. You can use them to mop up spills, wash your face, clean your hands, take sponge baths, treat your boots, and brush the mud off your clothes. They also work well as toilet paper, and even as ashtrays in a pinch. Baby-wipes rock.

Speaking of firsts, I saw something I thought was

rather clever in one of the bathrooms there. As you know, most of the local houses and many of the hotels in these regions have squat toilets, the Asian ones that are level with the floor, with a place to put your feet on either side. Many Western trekkers, and in particular those who are enjoying their 'golden years', find these low toilets uncomfortable and difficult to use, especially if they are beset with knee problems. As a result, some of the innkeepers have also installed a few Western-style toilets in their hotels to make the stiff-kneed visitors more comfortable. I have chosen lodges on the basis of this very amenity more than once.

However, replacing one of these Asian toilets can involve some major bathroom remodeling. So instead of going to all the trouble and expense of doing that, this discerning innkeeper had taken one of those standard, white plastic chairs that every hotel, lodge, café, restaurant, inn, tea stand, and bar in the world seems to have a generous supply of, and cut most of the bottom out of it. This modified chair was sitting in the corner of the toilet compartment. The idea was that if guests did not want to use the squat toilet, they could just place the plastic chair over it and sit on that instead. Ingenious. Simple. Effective. Economical. I thought I should try out this contraption for the record, but the need to use it never arose. That product review will have to wait until a return trip. Watch this space.

24

Boast not thyself of tomorrow,
For thou knowest not what a day may bring forth.

Proverbs 27:1

The so-called 'descent' through the region below Chame also began in fog and drizzle. The season was certainly living up to its long-standing reputation. The more arid sections of the Annapurna Massif shielded in the rain shadow higher up were now well behind me, and I was back in the full-on downpour zone. The first three hours of this stage contained about equal amounts of uphill trudging and gentler downhill sections, until about noon when the path plunged over a long, steep cliff face with wet, slippery footing. Trails in the Himalayas are not known for being especially accommodating, as we have seen.

As I shuffled along in the rain and the mud, it occurred to me that this day was unfolding very much like the last one, almost a photocopy. Yesterday, at about this same time, I had been doing the same thing, in the same conditions, in the same type of surroundings. This reflection triggered a bit of a daydream about the rather forgettable nature of so many of the days we live. When you stop and think about it, there isn't that much about most of our days that distinguishes any one of them from another. This is often as true of long-distance walking as it is of managing the usual, humdrum, daily grind. On a typical day, we climb out of bed, take a shower, imbibe a shot or two of caffeine and maybe a little breakfast, go to work, follow the regular schedule doing the same kinds of things in the same locations, have lunch, drive home, rustle up some dinner, blob out on the couch in front of the TV for a while, and finally head off to bed. Then we get up the next day and do pretty much all of the same things again in the same order. There are hundreds of days like this, making it nearly impossible to remember any particular one of them. With the passage of time, they all meld together into the long blur we call *the past*.

However, there are some days that really do stand out, days that are very different than all of the other more habitual ones. For most of us, there are only a few days like this in a whole lifetime, and they are unforgettable. On days of this sort, completely unexpected things can happen, things that radically change your life, events that shape your character and mold your psychology permanently. It is surely a blessing that such days don't occur too often. There is only so much shaping and molding that most people can cope with. Not for nothing is that ancient Chinese proverb about living in interesting times. Predictable, boring routines may be more of an advantage than we tend to think.

As you know, and may well have experienced personally, college campuses have long been hotbeds of drinking to excess. This has been the case for many centuries all over the world. When I was a university student, we were very much part of this long-established tradition. Our set, which means me and Kendra, my best friend, rented simple rooms in a cheap boarding house close to campus, with a communal kitchen on the ground floor, and an overgrown, weed patch of a backyard where we stacked our empty El

Cheapo gallon jugs. In plain English, the two of us were basically winos who also attended some classes, not infrequently with substantial hangovers.

One afternoon, as we were sitting on the upstairs landing sipping away as usual, a small, white car pulled up to the front of the house. A somewhat scruffy young man was promptly shoved out onto the lawn, a battered, plastic suitcase was unceremoniously heaved after him, and the woman at the wheel stomped on the gas and blasted off. In short, she straight out dumped him, literally and emotionally.

Greatly distraught, he barged angrily into the house cursing and shouting, and dropped his suitcase in the hallway outside his new room close to where we were sitting. He yanked the suitcase open, rummaged around in it furiously for a moment or two, and whipped out a bundle of love letters tied with a green ribbon. Cursing and shouting unabated, he started savagely tearing them up and strewing the fragments all over the landing, completely oblivious of the two amazed strangers silently and incredulously looking on. And then, after a few moments of this, he burst into tears, and began crawling around frantically on his hands and knees, trying to piece the scraps back together, calling loudly for Scotch tape, sobbing profusely.

While this performance was in progress, we remained there in shock, wondering just what sort of a whack job was moving in with us. After an interval, when he had calmed down somewhat, he took his disordered suitcase and what was left of the mangled letters into his room, and finally introduced himself. His name was Julius. As the air cleared, we began to feel sorry for him. After all, he had just been roundly kicked out and dramatically abandoned. He was obviously heartbroken, and taking it pretty hard. We introduced ourselves in turn, and tried to make him feel better. We helped him pick up the shreds of paper that were still scattered across the floor, thinking he would get over this setback once some water had passed under the bridge. And, since our go-to solution for practically every wrinkle in life was *have a glass of wine*, we handed him one. This turned out to be a major blunder.

When Julius drank alcohol, even if it was only a small amount, his behavior quickly became really, really bizarre. He started doing things we had never heard of, or could ever have imagined. He would sprawl on his bed with his door open, moaning loudly and calling out my name, claiming he was dying. He would collapse on the floor at the bottom of the stairs with his neck cocked at a strange angle, pretending that he had just broken it in a fall. On more than one occasion, he exploded into violent rampages, shouting and screaming and smashing windows, and then charged off into the night, and came back in a police car in the wee hours. We began to see why he had been so emphatically dumped when he arrived. This Julius fellow was a serious piece of work, and any sort of drinking with him was absolutely the wrong thing to do. His very extraordinary and highly alarming weirdness became so constant and so unmanageable, one day we sat him down in the kitchen and plainly told him that we would not drink with him ever again, period. And we meant it.

Once we understood what we were actually dealing with and what we could expect, the *no drinking with Julius* policy continued in earnest for about six weeks or so. Then Kendra, my constant companion and one true friend and drinking buddy came to the decision that it was time for her to transfer to another school to pursue a real career in nursing. She had had enough of just drifting aimlessly through one university term and into another without any sort of clear, practical goal. We had been close mates for several years. This was going to be a major change for us.

Near to the time of her departure, we got together in my room for a farewell party. We were sitting around on the floor, some sentimental string music was playing on the boom box, we were unhappy about the impending parting of the ways, and the daily gallon was ebbing fast. Julius, who was lying around in the room next door, knew we were in there, he knew that we were drinking, and he also knew that we did not want to drink with him. Nonetheless, he went down to the kitchen and put together a large tray of party snacks, dips, olives, chips, chopped vegetables, and the like. Then he carried this generous spread up the stairs, and gently pushed open my unlocked door.

At this juncture, we were well into our cups, we were feeling quite sad, and the touching strings played on. In this condition, we just didn't have the heart to tell him to leave. He had a highly insinuating way of making us pity him. We should have shown some better judgement here after all the repeated examples of his extreme behavior in the past, but we welcomed him anyway, and poured him an ample glass of wine. And, as we really should have expected, things quickly unraveled from there.

A short while later, he was sitting next to me on the floor with his arm around my shoulders, hand-feeding me assorted tidbits from the tray, and flaunting a horrible, insidious grin. A force of sheer evil was flowing through him to me. He was channeling something truly awful, and suddenly I just snapped. Something in the core of my being reacted violently: I was not having any more of this. I lurched up and threw him out of the room, and then crashed out of the house. I knocked around in a nearby public park in great inner turmoil for some hours until the sun came up, and then I got out on the road to hitch-hike to the Pacific coast about fifty miles away. I really needed a long walk outdoors to recover from this thoroughly poisonous collision.

I arrived at the coast on a blustery winter's day. Long shafts of sunlight were mixing with dark showers and stiff gusts coming in off the churning ocean, with shimmering rainbows flaring into view and fading away at short intervals. I walked along by the water's edge for about twenty minutes, and then I came to a dead stand, abruptly aware of something that was entirely beyond all of my previous experience. My fullest attention had just been seized by an overwhelmingly majestic, unearthly presence shining in the clouds a mile or two offshore above the rumbling waves. I felt like a cockroach on a kitchen floor must feel when the lights suddenly come on in the middle of the night. I stood there petrified, deeply stunned by an awesome, dread-inspiring force beaming towards me.

This was not something I was seeing with my

physical eyes. It was also far more than just a feeling. This was the seeing and perceiving you do with the third eye. It was a highly telepathic moment: I immediately recognized what it was. This was a gleam of communication from above. However, it was not about sweetness and blessing. It was not about joy and peace. On the contrary, this was the upper world bluntly informing me in the most no-nonsense manner that I was weighed in the balances and found wanting, warning me to examine my ways. This mesmerizing indictment was instantly and unmistakably clear and obvious, a flash of perfect understanding. If it had been spelled out in huge, bold letters on some vast screen, it could not have been more starkly plain.

My response was three-fold: a) I stammered out a jumbled, halting acknowledgement that was intended to mean *point taken*; b) I timidly said *please show me what to do*; and then, c) shaken to the core, I fled. I scrambled up the embankment back on to the coast highway, stuck out my thumb, and jumped into the first car that stopped without asking where it was going. Anywhere but there was fine with me. The shock from all this slowly diminished as our distance from that windy beach increased, but I had no idea what a thorough re-education that parting request was going to produce down the line. This close encounter of the third kind wasn't over yet. However, as Scheherazade said to the Shah on a thousand nights running, that is another story for another day.

Reviewing what I have written here, it occurs to me that I have not managed to recount this event very effectively. This unsought-for interview on the sand lasted only a few minutes, and it happened long ago. That day was so fraught, and this experience was so far beyond the pale, and such a complete surprise, I just don't have the right words to describe what is probably the most intense and piercing moment of my life. Before we turn the page on this chapter, I will just reiterate that it is no doubt for the best that days like this one do not befall too often. I don't think I could handle very many of them.

25

*A whole is that which has a beginning,
a middle, and an end.*

Aristotle

The next destination was the small village of Chamje, which is not to be confused with the similar-sounding Chame above it. To get there I had to pass through another section of towering cliffs, streaming waterfalls, and steep, unnerving drop-offs. Although this lush, well-watered area contains some of the most strikingly beautiful parts of the whole circuit, the phenomenal precipices were making me more than a little wary and uneasy. Despite all the mountain walking I have done, I am still afraid of heights. I stayed close to the inner wall of the track.

I remembered Chamje from a previous walk undertaken during the years of the Maoist unrest. In former times, some of the villages in this region had been toll stations for the old rice-for-salt trade routes conducted with yaks and goats across the high passes in the Manang region into Tibet. Those ancient routes have now been shut down by the Chinese, but the tradition of collecting tolls was still alive and well, as I was about to find out. On that other trip, my anxious guide had quietly stepped up to my table during the afternoon tea break, and whispered with great urgency: *Get your pack and follow me. We need to leave immediately.*

Knowing him to be a man of truth and reliability, I did what he asked without questioning right away. When we were back on the trail beyond the town, he explained that the men who were sitting at another table across from us in the tea house were Maoist fighters. He told me he had overheard them making plans to start demanding money from the hotel guests at gunpoint a few minutes later. There really are some major advantages to walking with the local people.

I had arrived in Chamje several hours ahead of schedule. This was no doubt the effect of coming down from the heights of the recent weeks. By now I was several thousand vertical meters lower than the area near Thorung La. There was much more oxygen in the air here. To cope with the thinner air higher up, your body produces a large quantity of extra red blood cells in order to collect more O2 in your lungs. Then when you drop down into lower elevations, these extra cells are still working, and this gives you an abnormally rich blood oxygen level. That, in addition to now being twenty-five pounds lighter and considerably more fit, puts a real spring in your step as you descend. And, of course, gravity is also working with you going in this direction.

I had expected to get there sometime in the late afternoon and call it a day, but it was now only a bit after lunchtime. I stationed myself at an outside table in front of a convenient lodge (the very same one that had the Maoist 'tax collectors') to have a break and a drink and ponder what to do next. This establishment was under the skillful management of an especially well-organized and charming Nepali girl about thirteen or fourteen years old who spoke perfect English. She must have been a very young child during my former visit. She had the place thoroughly in hand; everything in sight was immaculate. The copper pots hanging on the walls were glowing brightly, the napkins were perfectly folded and stacked, the menus and the flowers on the tables were becomingly arranged, all the windows were spotless, and the floors and the porches were freshly swept. Everything about the place spoke of high order and efficiency.

She was also as sharp as the proverbial tack. As I sat there trying to decide whether to stop for the day or to press on, she read my mind. She told me to sit tight while she looked into arranging a ride to carry me down the mountain. And sure enough, about half an hour later, an empty jeep pulled up at my table, and she motioned for me to get in: *He's going all the way to Besi Sahar*, she announced, with a bright and endearing smile. When you are trying to find transportation in the East, you quickly learn to accept whatever is available, whenever it is available. I thanked her, and climbed in. As the jeep rolled away from the lodge, I was thinking that whoever had the good fortune to marry her would be a very blessed man indeed. As Colonel Brandon says of Willoughby in *Sense and Sensibility: May he endeavor to deserve her.*

What followed was probably the most battering ride I have ever taken in a motor vehicle. These lower sections of the Annapurna 'road' should be on the list of the hardest places to drive in the world. About ten percent of it is a minimal but fairly negotiable mountain track. On the rest, roughly a third of it is basically a stream bed full of rapidly flowing water, another third consists of long sloughs of thick mud, and what's left is drifts of loose stones and boulders, and narrow, irregular shelves of bedrock sticking out of the cliffs hard by. Riding in that thing was like being in a tiny boat on a heaving ocean. We careened and we pitched from end to end, and we rocked and we rolled from side to side, gears grinding up and down non-stop as we repeatedly plowed across small ponds and struggled through axle-swallowing stretches of deep muck. I had to hold on with both hands the whole way.

If I had known back in Chamje that the ride was going to be like this, I would have remained at that peaceful, welcoming oasis and just walked down the next day. However, as my passage here below has so often demonstrated, judgement comes from experience, and experience comes from lack of judgement, as an apt saying rather neatly expresses it. By the by, Annapurna is well along in the process of sluffing off this narrow, rapidly eroding track. Without lots of ongoing maintenance and repairs, this rugged path probably wouldn't be much more than a fading memory in about another generation or so.

All things come to a close, as we are told. I arrived

in Besi Sahar around sunset, extremely relieved to be done with that body-slamming jeep ride at long last. I checked in to the first hotel I came to, and not having the energy to go out and track down a likely-looking restaurant, I repaired to the balcony outside my room and dined on the local whisky and potato chips. And then it was promptly and directly to bed after a memorable albeit rather bruising day. I lay down gratefully under the rasping ceiling fan in my small room, and this round of walking in the hills was at an end.

26

*The follies of youth are in retrospect glorious,
compared to the follies of old age.*

G.K. Chesterton (attributed)

I was down from the mountain. Now came the long drive back to the capital. I went out on the street early the next morning and found a minibus heading for Kathmandu. These basic vehicles are small, and packed to the absolute, Nepalese max, but they are fast. They will get you where you need to go quickly and inexpensively. I stuffed myself into the child-sized space as well as I could, braced for the shrill music and the grating horn, and looked out the window at the monsoon-drenched land.

Since the trip out, the rice had grown considerably. Fields that had been water and mud back then were now a lovely, brilliant green. Thickets of bougainvillea and hibiscus lit up the roadsides and adorned the walls in radiant cascades of purple and red. However, when we left the cultivated, rural areas, the transition to the scenes of poverty along the main highway was a stark one. Most of the people existing on the side of the tarmac were just camping out in basic bamboo shanties with mud floors, surrounded by rusting, abandoned machinery, broken pieces of infrastructure, and crumbling, jerry-built buildings. Large sections of the road were unpaved. Thick layers of swirling, clinging dust stirred by the relentless floods of traffic had settled on nearly everything in sight, and there were seas of trash in every direction. Life beside the highway is harsh.

And yet, in the midst of all this manifest hardship, there were colorful splashes of vitality and gladness. As we continued on, we were passing processions of jubilant villagers decked out in dazzling red and gold silks, draped with multiple garlands of newly picked flowers. They were accompanied by enthusiastic, horn-blowing and drum-whacking minstrels and strings of smiling, well-scrubbed children walking along the road in their Sunday best. Someone near me on the bus said these gatherings were wedding parties. The astrologers must have announced that this was an auspicious day to get married. A succession of these colorful spectacles brightened the cloudy day.

There was something moving about these joyful little parades. It was touching to see these unassuming, hard-pressed people emerge so cheerfully in such blazing finery to celebrate a special event. As I looked out at these delighted crowds, the contrast between their way of doing a wedding and my own wedding day, which had no lively musicians, no boisterous fanfare, no blazing finery, no garlands of sunny flowers, and no bands of happy children, could not have been greater. What were we thinking back there, anyway?

Not very much, actually, if I remember it correctly. I had arrived back in Turkey once again after a long spell of traveling in some of the countries farther East, vaguely thinking about going back to college to complete my degree. However, at this stage I had no clear plans as yet, and hardly any money, so I took a job teaching English in a language school in the suburbs of Istanbul to make ends meet while I considered how best to proceed. This school was a pleasant and agreeable place to work. The students were very respectful and focused, I enjoyed being there, and I was fitting in quite nicely.

And then I did something dumb. One day, as I was getting off the commuter train near the school, a fellow passenger handed me a small theological pamphlet. I thanked him in my rudimentary Turkish, and walked on towards the school examining it. When I arrived in my room, I put it down on the teacher's desk and started getting the day's course work underway. In the middle of the class, a student sitting at a table about five feet away from mine noticed the little brochure and asked to see it. Instead of taking the two steps to his desk and handing it to him, I gently tossed it over and carried on.

This was not the right thing to do. No one there said anything, the class ended normally, and I went home as usual. But the next day, as I was making my way to my classroom, the director stepped into the hall and quietly invited me into his office. There, without preamble or any sort of explanation whatsoever, I was handed my wages and summarily shown to the door. I was back on the sidewalk in less than five minutes. Surprised and bewildered, I wandered slowly back towards the station, wondering what could have happened. And then I remembered that leaflet from the day before. Even though this incident happened quite innocently, I had inadvertently committed a sensitive cultural affront.

As a result, I was now out of a job, and at a loose end once again. As it happened, a fellow traveler with two small children and a stack of luggage was moving down to the Aegean city Izmir that week, and she needed some help taking the overnight bus ride south. I offered to assist her, and this suggestion was welcomed. I rode with them on the bus to Izmir, helped them move everything over to her friends' residence, and then hit the couch after a long, wakeful night, intending to get back on the bus and return to Istanbul in the evening.

However, fate had other ideas. Several hours later, when I was getting up, a beautiful Turkish girl walked into the apartment. Aysel was a friend of the family and a frequent visitor. We started chatting over the customary tulip-shaped glasses of black tea, and soon found ourselves becoming rather enchanted by one another. These days love at first sight is widely considered to be nothing more than a romantic myth, but there it was.

Over the course of the next few weeks, the enchantment continued and intensified, and it wasn't very long before we were both pretty well bewitched.

In this condition it is not too unusual for rationality to go out the window, and our powerful feelings quickly took over. I knew hardly any Turkish, she spoke only a little English, and we did not know each other at all. Even so, now thoroughly enamored, within a few weeks we had concocted a reckless plan to elope to Europe and get married there. Aysel set about obtaining a passport, and I looked into the ferries that made crossings over to Greece. The follies of youth are glorious.

The preparations for our departure proceeded apace, and one morning in mid-April we nervously got on a minibus bound for the small port of Chesme an hour or so down the coast from Izmir. The small ferry from there to the Greek island of Chios didn't leave until four o'clock in the afternoon, so we had to spend some long, anxious hours lying low in an obscure tea shop on one of the quiet back streets. In these close-knit parts, you never know when a relative or a family acquaintance might happen by. About half an hour before the ferry was scheduled to depart, we plucked up our drooping courage and went over to the harbor to go through the border formalities and get on the boat.

The departure was fraught. It so happened that my tourist visa had expired a few days earlier. As we have already seen, overstaying one's visa in some of these lands is not really a good idea. I tried hard not to think about that as the officials processed my passport. Another factor ramping up the already ample tension was that at this time, the military was governing Turkey, and the Air Force was in charge of the national borders. One phone call back to headquarters asking for advice about what to do with us could possibly have landed me in a formidable Turkish prison for a lengthy round of the *Midnight Express* experience. Fortunately, nothing untoward happened, and a few minutes later we boarded the ferry uneventfully. It left on time, and as it chugged away from the pier and out into the Aegean, multiple waves of indescribable relief washed over us.

At this point, the plan was to head for Gretna Green, the village on the Scottish border where the town officials will marry pretty much anybody with no questions asked, as I had heard. Getting there would involve a seriously uncomfortable, two-and-a-half-day Magic Bus ride from Athens to Holland, and then another ferry trip from there across the Channel. It was going to be a very long and exhausting journey, but we just didn't have the means to do anything better at that point. In the event, this journey took even longer than we had anticipated.

The best laid schemes o' mice and men gang aft a-gley, as the well-known and beloved poet from Scotland once phrased it.

After two sleepless nights on the bus, followed by another one on the ferry, we finally disembarked in England, no doubt looking rather the worse for wear. My haggard appearance was probably a factor in what happened next: On the way through customs and passport control, a brusque border official put me through a far more extensive grilling than I was expecting, and he then examined my small backpack very meticulously. In the course of this thorough search, he came across my journal containing numerous, detailed descriptions of my recent travels and adventures out in the East. He flicked through it for a moment, and then he sat down at his desk to peruse it more fully.

Although I was not exactly a man of fashion at this point, I was wearing decent clothes, and I was reasonably clean-cut. I did not look like a hippie. Nevertheless, when he stood up from his reading, it was pretty clear that he had made up his mind that we were persona non grata. I politely explained to him, with complete honesty, that all we intended to do was go up to Gretna Green, get a marriage license, and then fly on to the States as soon as possible. I was entirely truthful and up front about our itinerary, and I believed that we had enough money to do this if we went about it conservatively.

But he wasn't buying it. He said we were too underfunded for the plan we had presented, and then he had us escorted back on to the ferry for the return trip to Holland. When we eventually arrived there after yet another sleepless night, the border officials on that side directed us into a small cell just outside of passport control. At this point we were not in England or in Holland. We were now stuck in legal no man's land between the two countries. Needless to say, this is a very awkward and messy place to be, as Tom Hanks so graphically discovers in *Terminal*. Fortunately, a fraying notebook contained the phone number of some friends currently living in the Netherlands. When these border officials contacted them, they managed to convince them that we were harmless, and they graciously took on full financial responsibility for us as well. The officials relented, and stamped us into the country.

I spent the summer working at a factory in Utrecht loading canal barges with construction gravel and sand. A few months later, when we had assembled enough funds, we took a train over to the small town of Tønder on the Danish/German border, which is more or less the Gretna Green of Denmark. The town hall officials registered us on Monday, and then married us the following Thursday with a short, elegant ceremony featuring six-foot candle sticks, long, black robes, and a solemn address on the serious nature of matrimony. In addition, they provided us with an impressive, internationally recognized marriage license that was written in seven languages and handsomely embossed with the town seal. (One of these languages was actually Turkish, which proved to be very helpful later on.)

With this handsome new document now to hand, we returned to Holland, obtained a visa for the US, boarded a cheap flight to JFK, and continued onward from there to my former college town to complete my degree. It had certainly been a more involved and harrowing adventure than we had planned for, and certainly nowhere near as colorful as the Nepali approach, but things did all work out in the end. Holland really and truly deserves its long-standing reputation as an oasis of liberality and a bastion of tolerance and decency. My sincere and abiding thanks to that wonderful country.

27

In Mintirib there are some dunes
Made of orange sand;
Where the sun beats down day after day,
And there's not a soul at hand.
An ancient shrine sits crumbling here,
Its roof is on the ground;
Thistles its only faithful,
The wind its only sound.
Late in the day I sheltered there,
As the sun was sinking;
Orange light on the orange sand,
Shutting down my thinking.
The camels appear one by one,
Each in its own good time;
And vanish silently into the dunes,
Their footprints a long, thin line.

Oman desert meditation

I was both relieved and stressed to be back in the big city. I was more than ready to take a break from the hardships of the trail, and looking forward to a hot bath, a much-needed cleanup, and some decent food. My eagerness for the noise, the crowds, the traffic, the pollution, and the all-night disco music was somewhat more moderate.

I checked back into the friendly and welcoming hotel where my extra luggage was stored, and then got on with the standard return to civilization occupations. First things first, I went into a restaurant and requested a 'sizzler'. A sizzler is a cast-iron pan of meat and vegetables super-heated in a broiler. This was the first non-rice and eggs dinner I had eaten for some weeks. As the waiters were bringing it over to my table, they poured a cup of Kukri rum on it and set it alight. When this dish arrived at my table, it was not only sizzling vigorously, it was also fully ablaze. Now there is a fine way to keep down the giardia, I said to myself, and why didn't I think of that? I have been lugging liters of tax-free rum and brandy all over the place in my pack for many years. But then again, your usual garden variety of restaurant workers might not take kindly to customers who go around lighting up their orders.

Fortified as I was by this long-overdue square

meal, the rest of the post-trek decompression proceeded apace. I went to town, as it were. I fished out some clean clothes and brought everything else to a laundry service down the street. I took a long, steamy shower and cut off the frayed and blackened agglomerations of medical tape and bandages on my battered feet. I rounded up some tangerines and apples from the street vendors, the first fresh fruit I had seen for many days. I bought a small bottle of real mouthwash, and several other bottles of extra-strong Nepal Ice beer. And lastly, I went to a barber shop to get a professional shave to remove the by now solidly established Robinson Crusoe look. It is very difficult to take off a tough trail beard with a disposable, plastic razor. It just bounces off. What you really need for this is a barber wielding a well-stropped, old-fashioned straight razor.

Another part of the coming-down-from-the-trail ritual is to look at the headlines and check your messages. I turned on the TV in my room and watched the news for a bit. The country I was heading for next was now undergoing some regional upheavals and street protests, but it still appeared to have a viable government, and there were no other major surprises or unusual happenings anywhere else to speak of. The world was more or less the same, and about as ineffectually and haphazardly managed as it was before I had started walking. However, the messages did contain an unexpected development. While I had been wandering up in the hills, the airline had cancelled some of my onward flights. Sorting that out was going to require taking a trip downtown.

After breakfast the following morning, I headed over to the airline office, which was several kilometers away. I was not pleased about the cancelled flights. Life really is fraught with inconvenience some of the time. However, as I made my way along the crowded streets, I realized that this was another opportunity to acquire merit by learning patience, and not to bemoan such things unduly. And this is a common feature of modern travel, after all. Getting around in our busy, thickly populated times does sometimes involve this sort of minor annoyance, but it isn't really all that strenuous or difficult. About all you ever have to do is print your boarding pass and head to the airport, and within a just few hours you are whisked away to almost anywhere in the world. Now and again things may get slightly more complicated, like today, when you might have to actually go see an agent in person, but most traveling these days is usually pretty cut and dried. Sitting on an airplane may not be very colorful or memorable, but it is efficient. How different this is from the way things were a century or two, or even just fifty or sixty years, ago. The nature of travel has definitely changed.

Robinson Crusoe's beard brings to mind a curious benchmark for this. Some years back, I was browsing around the shelves of the public library in a college town in Maine. I came across a section of materials touching on Central Asia and the Great Game that was afoot in some of the territories north of India about a hundred and fifty years ago. At the time, the history of that region was unfamiliar to me. This neglected-looking collection nicely filled in a number of the gaps with captivating descriptions of the main events and personalities of that colorful period.

In the mid-nineteenth century, most of the major nations of Europe were energetically engaged in empire acquisition. At that time, ongoing and completely unscrupulous land grabbing was the standard operating procedure, and it was happening all over the map. The Czar of Russia, who was fully dedicated to this world vision, was attempting to expand his domains southwards into Central Asia. The British were concerned that the Russians might also have further designs on India, and thus the Great Game got underway.

In order to circumvent Russian expansion in

that direction, the British were interested in forming a defensive alliance with the rulers of Khiva, Bokhara, and Khokand, some of the sheikhdoms to the north of Afghanistan in what is now Uzbekistan. To explore the possibilities of this sort of arrangement, several officers were sent to this region to meet with the rulers there during the early 1840s. One of the first of the envoys dispatched on this mission was Colonel Charles Stoddart, who was followed a short time later by Captain Arthur Conolly.

In the event, Nasrullah Khan, the Emir of Bokhara, proved to be a rather unsavory despot who was disinclined towards British interests. He had these officers thrown into some seriously nasty dungeons. When news of this became public back in England a few months later, there was considerable outrage that Her Majesty's ambassadors were being treated so shamefully. However, the British government was not quite sure how to handle the situation. The area was very remote, and with memories of the recent and disastrous First Afghan War fresh in their minds, they were not keen to send in an army to rescue the officers and school the Emir on the error of his ways.

While they were thinking about what to do, up stepped pillar of the fringe Reverend Joseph Wolff, a fairly obscure Church of England clergyman from

Surrey. This most unlikely hero volunteered to travel to Bokhara and attempt to get the officers released. Other than just being willing to go, his rather scant qualifications for the job were that he had been to Bokhara and had met the Emir on a previous round of Central Asian wanderings some years earlier. With nothing much else on the table just then, the government decided to let him try it, and assisted him in assorted ways, including providing him with an official letter of introduction to the court of the Ottoman Sultan of Turkey.

Reverend Wolff traveled to Turkey, and with some further help from the powers, assembled a befitting caravan and set out on the long, perilous road to Central Asia. This arduous journey took many weeks, and while he was on the way, Nasrullah Khan had these unfortunate officers publicly executed. When Reverend Wolff arrived in Bokhara, he was too late. For a time, it looked like he was heading for the same fate as Stoddard and Conolly. However, as it turned out, the Emir found him completely ridiculous and a source of great hilarity, and eventually let him go unharmed.

The reason for mentioning this little history is not just to rehearse a distant episode of the Great Game; the point here is Reverend Wolff's luggage. Along with a lot of other things, the Reverend Wolff's baggage train included a sizeable pile of copies of *Robinson Crusoe* translated into Arabic to distribute as gifts to the various potentates and headmen met along the way. This is assuredly a style of traveling you probably won't find anywhere these days. Who would think it was expedient to go anyplace with camel-loads of *Robinson Crusoe* today?

Another benchmark concerning the changing nature of travel that I found in that same library was a bit more disheartening. Some weeks later, while I was pottering around in those same shelves once again, I discovered another volume that sparked my deep interest immediately. This book described shipping companies that operated cargo freighters to smaller, out-of-the-way ports in various parts of the world. These ships traveled slowly on voyages that could take anywhere from three to six months, following a variety of different routes. For a modest fee, you would be provided with a basic, private cabin containing a bed, a closet, a desk, a port hole, and a bathroom, and you took your meals with the ship's crew in the dining room. The system was, you put your name on the waiting list for the route of your choice, and when a berth became available, the company would then ring you up and ask if you wanted to go. If you did, you paid the moderate fare, packed your bag, and sailed away over the horizon.

The routes these ships followed were very appealing to me. For example, one of these trips started in Baltimore, crossed the Atlantic, went through the Mediterranean and the Red Sea, and then steamed slowly down the east coast of Africa delivering cargo at assorted harbors there for several months. On another route, a ship left from New York, and ambled in a leisurely fashion down the coast of South America to Argentina. And one of the longer voyages began in Savannah or New Orleans, transited the Panama Canal, and then spent six full months calling at various small islands all the way to Australia. When the ships arrived in their ports of call, they usually had to wait for a few days or possibly weeks for their turn to unload at the simple facilities. During this waiting-to-dock period, the passengers were free to go ashore and explore at will.

I was thrilled. My traveler's imagination was thoroughly fired. What a brilliant way to spend a long window between jobs! This was definitely something I wanted to try. I took the book home, installed myself by the phone, and called up all of the companies that were listed. I wanted to enroll on all the waiting lists that were available. However, to my not inconsiderable surprise and dismay, all of the companies that I contacted told me the same thing: *I am sorry, Sir. We no longer operate that service. We do not accept those passengers any more.*

When I asked why not, they all said the same thing as well. One after another, the people on the phone politely explained that they had been sued too many times by some of the passengers they had signed on.

I couldn't believe it. Sued for what, might one ask? A passenger goes ashore in, say, Zanzibar, tries a bit of the street food, gets diarrhea, and then sues the shipping company for 'discomfort'? Or, the ship had to wait to unload its cargo slightly longer than expected somewhere, and a passenger went home and sued the company for 'inconvenience'? I really wondered about this. I hoped all of this suing had not been for 'reasons' as shallow and so petty as these, but almost anything is possible in such litigious times as the present one. And really, if someone cannot handle a touch of diarrhea, or a little delay, what on earth are they doing on a slow boat to Africa in the first place? I was truly disappointed that such an affordable style of classic, long-range travel was now gone with the wind.

Later on, it occurred to me that even if such passages were still available now, it is quite possible they might not be as inspiring or as colorful as they were previously. Today, these ships would presumably not be the sort of smaller, aging tramp steamers that the likes of Tintin and Captain Haddock might have boarded in the 1930s, with open decks to stroll and a convenient rail to lean on while you gazed dreamily out to sea smoking your pipe. In our times, these freighters would most likely be larger container ships, and you would probably find yourself buried in a deep well of shipping containers somewhere near the back of the boat. Also, with more modernized facilities, the turnaround times in the ports would be a lot shorter as well, and you might not get the opportunity to explore nearly as much. It is likely that this just wouldn't be the same kind of journey now. The romance of travel has definitely taken a major hit in these days of super-efficiency and computerized operations.

28

The use of traveling is to regulate imagination by reality.

Samuel Johnson

What would be a suitable birthday present for an aging parent who already has just about everything? This question was on my mind when I stepped out for some coffee the next morning. After the coffee, I poked around in the curio shops on the back streets near my hotel looking for something appropriate to send to my mother in Vermont. And suddenly there it was right in front of me: an ancient, rosewood cane forgotten in a dusty corner of a small junk store. This was a skillfully worked piece of rustic craftsmanship, with a lovely patina accrued during long use on untold village paths.

The post office that handled international shipping was a fair way off in a different section of town, so I went back out into the streets once again. Arriving at the overseas shipping window sometime later, I spent about two hours going through a mailing procedure that was even more antique than the cane itself. First, there were some hard-to-read forms, printed in dim Nepalese script on pink pages with tiny spaces to write your information. A kindly post office worker sheltering under a canvas tarp outside in the garden (this was still the rainy season) helped me complete those.

When the forms had been duly filled in, two customs officers took the cane and spent a good thirty minutes wrapping and packing it very meticulously. They rummaged about in a sizeable pile of old boxes and plastic that I had taken to be the trash heap, and pulled out a well-worn fragment of bubble wrap. They fixed this around the cane with generous amounts of masking tape, and then they covered it with a thick layer of cardboard gleaned from the same pile. When the cardboard was firmly secured, one of the officers sat down at a small table off to one side with a needle and thread and painstakingly hand-sewed a cotton sleeve for it. When this was ready, he inserted the cane, and slowly and carefully stitched it shut.

This work of art was passed back to me to write the address, and then it was handed on to the nearby sealing-wax man. The sealing-wax man put a bar of red wax into a candle, making a mess on the floor next to his low stool, and daubed little globs of wax onto the seams in a dozen or more places. He then impressed each of these red globs with a small, brass customs seal, one after another. Then came some further hard-to-read forms, a visit to the weighing station, the long line at the cashier's desk, and finally off it went, looking very official and important indeed. Brits in the days of the Raj sent and received parcels that were packed like this. Unexpectedly finding yourself in time bubbles like this one is certainly among the abiding charms of traveling in this region.

With the cane on its way in capable hands, I ambled back through the bazaar towards my hotel. Along the way, I watched a truly insidious begging operation in progress in the cloth and textile area. There I came across a religious practitioner dressed in the usual holy man get-up: an orange cotton sarong with a matching orange headdress, a long-sleeved yellow shirt draped with the customary strings of dark beads made from dried rudraksha seeds, and plenty of war paint. This character put an ornate bronze bowl on a tray, filled it with generous handfuls of incense, and grazed it with a lighter a few times.

When the incense was properly burning, he carried this smudge pot into a nearby shop selling vibrant silks and beautiful, expensive fabrics. Using a scrap of cardboard he had retrieved from the gutter in front of the door, he then proceeded to fan clouds of thick, acrid smoke all around the shop, softly mumbling a repertoire of suitable blessings and texts as he went. The last thing any cloth merchant needs is to have his entire stock get smoked up with such nasty-smelling fumes, so he immediately gave this pushy charlatan a donation to go away. He left, and promptly stepped across to the next cloth shop close by, and repeated this same routine with the same results. Totally devious, but highly effective.

Techniques of this sort are practicable in places like Kathmandu because many of the cities in Asia still adhere to the old style of urban planning that clustered the same kinds of merchandise into designated zones. As a result, there will be some streets filled with stores that all trade in brassware, other streets specializing in stalls selling chickens (like 'Chicken Street' in Kabul), and still others containing long rows of textile shops, such as this one. These incense-wielding beggars love this ancient arrangement. They can just march down the line from one shop to the next, cleaning up as they go. A full quota of funds can rapidly and easily be gathered in a hundred yards.

This type of panhandling works here because the mentality of the population supports it. The unseen world is real and close to these folks. Propitiating the spirits is seen as an important thing to do in their view, in a way it just isn't farther West. Just imagine what might happen if you tried this incense performance in the fabric stores of New York. You would be doing exceptionally well if you were not tarred and feathered on the spot. Over here in the East, things are different. A wide variety of street and temple people make a livelihood of allegedly trafficking in things spiritual. There are armies of sadhus, pilgrims, spiritual guides, fakirs, meditation teachers, religious beggars, holy men, fortune tellers, mediums, and gurus thriving all over these lands, even on some of the highest and most remote trails in the back country.

This inclination is not just the preserve of quacks and religious con men, such as these incense crooks. Lots of everyday, mainstream types of people dabble in the occult in assorted ways as well. I once met some girls in Turkey who had created a hobby out of calling on unseen spirits in a sort of home-grown Ouija board type of activity. This was in the days before mobile phones and the internet were available, so they got into this as a form of entertainment. Many teenage girls in the East often have a lot less freedom than they do elsewhere. They are usually on very strict schedules that only allow them to go from home to school, or to work, and then back. All of their time is closely regulated, and their social contacts are carefully controlled.

In some countries, girls can be severely punished by their own family members for just talking with a male acquaintance on a bus. Although that is not generally the normal practice, this does happen. This sort of abiding *purdah* mentality is deeply rooted, underlying and directing many aspects of life you might not expect it to. For example, think of those graceful ankle bracelets that are widely seen throughout the East. These jingly, intricately devised ornaments have long been a highly popular form of traditional jewelry. One of their main, but not very often mentioned, purposes was to monitor the whereabouts and the movements of women, whether they were busy in the kitchen, working out in the garden, or eavesdropping behind the curtains. What we have there is a subtle instrument of refined control freakery disguised as de rigueur beauty and high fashion. This mindset is complex.

However, I digress. The point I was going to make was that in this ultra-supervised and constrained environment, there was not a lot for teenage girls to do. There wasn't much on TV other than a bit of news, some less than riveting agricultural development reports, and a few old movies. At that time, there were also no DVD players, no internet sites, and no social media. As such, they had to look for entertainment where they could, and dabbling in the spirit world seemed like an interesting possibility. In general, most girls who played with this sort of stuff only did so for a few years, experimenting with things like seances, trying to converse with departed relatives, and the like. But then as careers and marriages came along, they lost interest and moved on to other things. And, most of this so-called 'contact' was largely imaginary anyway.

But not always. Sometimes their attempts to contact the spirits of their departed relatives really worked, and a lot more successfully and dramatically than they expected. One of these girls in particular seemed to have a real gift in this area. The basic technique that she used was as follows: She would place a blank sheet of paper on the table in front of her, take a pencil loosely in her writing hand, and hold it upright on the paper. Then she would ask the spirit she wanted to talk to a question, and after a brief pause, her hand would start moving slowly and jerkily across the page, making long strings of connected scribblings that only she could understand. I think this has been called automatic writing somewhere. These long scribbles didn't look like anything meaningful at all, as if a small bird with ink on its feet had wandered back and forth across the paper a few times, but she could actually read them. To her, these wobbling, crabbed lines were coherent answers to her questions given in specific detail.

The first time I saw this happening, my hair stood on end. This was something right out of the horror movies. I had zero acquaintance with anything like that at all. However, after I had seen this procedure a few times, I calmed down. These messages were always expressed in gentle, reasonable language, and contained wise counsel and wholesome suggestions. When she was trying to choose between various courses of action, her responder provided helpful reminders and dis-recommended imprudent or unsound options. If something was lost, its location would be pointed out, and the like. After watching some of these exchanges, I decided that even though this activity was certainly out of the ordinary, it was probably harmless.

These things happened many years ago, and my memories are not crisp. But when I think back to that distant scene, my conclusion is that this operation was most probably the real deal. She could have made a fortune if she had wanted to set up a clairvoyant salon, but she wisely decided to keep all this to herself. It is also interesting to reflect that in today's device-rich world, she very possibly might never have discovered this talent at all. Instead, she would have been on her phone, chatting and messaging with her friends by day and by night, and this unusual pastime may never have developed.

29

Let me go climb those virgin snows,
And leave the dark stain of man behind;
Let me adventure, and heaven knows,
Grateful shall be my quiet mind.

Wilfrid Noyce

My journey was drawing to a close. I stayed on for several more days, catching up on my sleep, delighting in spreads of fiery tandoori cuisine, shopping around for a few more gifts, and organizing the souvenir-rich luggage. The monsoon was still in full swing, especially during the late afternoon. When it was pouring outside, I lingered in my room and read the novels of Jane Austen.

I was now the happy owner of a complete set of them. Books are wonderfully inexpensive in Kathmandu.

As I reflected on this tranquil, regenerating summer walking the soaring trails of Annapurna, a feeling of fulfillment and a sense of time well spent distilled over me. A lot of good things had happened. I rose from the couch, and turned off the ensnaring TV. I got out of the office, and forsook the stress-emitting screen it contains. I shed a substantial amount of painful, clogging weight, and, if not exactly the full flush of youth, I did regain a large measure of the fitness that had been lost in a long spell of highly sedentary living. I met many friendly, kind-hearted, and helpful people along the way: hotel workers, taxi drivers, rickshaw-wallahs, trail guides, shop owners, yak herdsmen, minibus men, fellow travelers, innkeepers, tea makers, village children. I had become less of a curmudgeon than I had been when I first arrived, and I had connected with the spirit of travel once again. After some long interludes of being housebound in a number of postings in parching, dust-blown deserts, I had been much refreshed by the splendid monsoon rains, and my heart had been uplifted and inspired by the vast panoramas of the untouched, eternal snows. I felt cleansed and fit and renewed.

In brief, visiting Nepal is good for you.

Bibliography

Austen, Jane. *Sense and Sensibility*. New York: Everyman's Library, Alfred A. Knopf, Inc., 1992. p. 174.

Bartlett's Familiar Quotations, 17th edn, edited by Justin Kaplan. New York: Little, Brown and Co., 2002.

G.K. Chesterton Quotes (Author of Orthodoxy). Goodreads https://www.goodreads.com/author/quotes/7014283.G_K_Chesterton.

Hertzog, Maurice. *Annapurna*. New York: Dutton, 1953.

Noyce, Wilfrid. *Climbing the Fish's Tail*. Heinemann: London, 1958.

Rodale, J.I. *The Synonym Finder.* New York: Grand Central Publishing, 1978.

Roget's International Thesaurus, 3rd edn, New York: Thomas Y. Crowell Company, 1962.

Slocum, Joshua. *Sailing Alone Around the World.* Project Gutenberg.

www.gutenberg.org/files/6317/6317-h/6317-h.htm. Chapter viii.

The Essential Haiku: Versions of Basho, Buson and Issa, edited by Robert Hass. Hopewell, New Jersey: The Ecco Press, 1994, p. 88.

The Holy Bible. Authorized King James Version, Holman Bible Publishers, Nashville, 1998.

The Oxford Book of Quotations, 2nd edn, edited by Geoffrey Cumberlege. London: Oxford University Press, 1953.

The Pacific Crest Trailside Reader; California, edited by Rees Hughes and Corey Lewis. Seattle: The Mountaineers Books, 2011. Chapter 44.

Trekking in the Nepal Himalaya, 8th edn, edited by Stan Armington. Footscray, Australia: Lonely Planet Publications Pty Ltd, 2001.

Wikipedia contributors. Annapurna Circuit [Internet]. *Wikipedia, The Free Encyclopedia*; 2019 Sep 22, 10:44 UTC [cited 2019 Sep 25].

Wikipedia contributors. Annapurna Conservation Area [Internet]. *Wikipedia, The Free Encyclopedia*; 2019 Sep 16, 21:46 UTC [cited 2019 Sep 25].

Wikipedia contributors. Annapurna Massif [Internet]. *Wikipedia, The Free Encyclopedia*; 2019 Sep 23, 18:57 UTC [cited 2019 Sep 25].

Wikipedia contributors. Thorong La [Internet]. *Wikipedia, The Free Encyclopedia*; 2019 Jul 31, 11:05 UTC [cited 2019 Sep 25].

Wolff, Joseph. *Narrative of a Mission to Bokhara, in the years 1843–1845, to Ascertain the Fate of Colonel Stoddart and Captain Conolly*. New York: Harper & Brothers, 1845.

Acknowledgements

I would like to offer my heartfelt thanks to everyone who assisted me in making this book a reality. First, very special thanks to the SilverWood Books team for accepting the project. Their thorough expertise, ongoing patience, and ready flexibility has made producing this my first book a very pleasant and educational process. In their skillful hands it rapidly evolved from a possible idea into a real work in progress. Without their input and guidance, this might well have remained a collection of trail-worn notebooks gathering dust somewhere in the bottom of my closet.

I am much obliged to Tim for his kind help getting my printer up and running, sorting out my patchy word-processing skills, and a raft of long-term technical support. I am grateful to Sibel for her generous help with the cover design, to Eva for her articulate and entertaining lexical advice, and to David for his permission to use his photographs of Nepal. Warm thanks to Tawanna, the kind stranger who gave me a pen in the bus station and enabled me to get some of these fleeting details down when mine had failed at a critical moment. And last but not least, a tip of the hat to the friends, colleagues, and relatives who suggested that I should take up this project in the first place.

www.ingramcontent.com/pod-product-compliance
Lightning Source LLC
Chambersburg PA
CBHW022101090426
42743CB00008B/673